The
PURPOSE
of
LIFE

28 POWERFUL, NEW KEYS FOR DISCOVERING
AND FULFILLING YOUR PURPOSE IN LIFE

By Dr. Daniel R. Condron

Library of Congress Control Number 2004117400

Library of Congress Cataloging in Publication Data
Condron, Daniel R.
     The Purpose of Life
     Summary: This book answers the most important questions of life,
why we are here and what is the purpose of life.

ISBN: 0-944386-35-0

© December, 2004 School of Metaphysics No. 100180
PRINTED IN THE UNITED STATES OF AMERICA

If you desire to learn more about the research and
teachings in this book, write to School of Metaphysics
World Headquarters, Windyville, Missouri 65783.
Or call us at 417-345-8411.
Visit us on the Internet at www.som.org
& www.peacedome.org

Any portion of **The Purpose of Life** may be reprinted or reproduced
in any form with the prior written permission of the Board of Governors of
the School of Metaphysics.

Table of Contents

Introduction

This is a book designed to give you the power to discover and fulfill your purpose in life.

To fulfill your purpose is to accomplish the most important thing you are here to do.

There are too many people walking around on the planet not knowing what they are here for or what they should be doing. This book answers those questions.

More importantly, this book tells you how to implement the information in order that it becomes knowledge, wisdom and enlightenment in your life.

A disciplined mind is required in order to know your purpose. Suggestions and instruction are given for gaining a disciplined mind.

There are 28 days in a true month. A real month is a lunar month. Thirteen months of 28 days each equals a year of 364 days, plus an extra day for peace, assimilation, and contemplation.

A lunar month is completed in 28 days. Most of the ancient peoples used a lunar month. In the present time, the lunar month is used in the almanac. Millions of people use this knowledge each year. The almanac is used for knowing when to plant gardens and crops.

The months of the solar calendar currently in use in the western world are not consistent. Some have 30 days others have 31.

By reading a chapter a day for one month of 28 days you will be in harmony with the lunar month and the natural rhythms of the universe.

After one month of reading this book and applying its powerful principles, you will better understand your purpose in life. What could be more powerful? Isn't that what you are here for?

Daniel R. Condron

The
PURPOSE
of
LIFE

Chapter One
The Purpose of Life

Understanding the Meaning of Life and Your Purpose in It

What is the purpose of life? This is the question people have asked since the beginning of recorded history and before recorded history.

Some people have searched to find the meaning of life. Other people have accepted the idea that a physical lifetime is only for the purpose of sensory experience. Others believe the purpose of life is to accumulate physical possessions.

Some individuals have discovered that there is more to life than meets the eye or any of the five senses. There is more to life than what a person sees, smells, hears, tastes and touches. These individuals have awakened to a higher truth and a greater reality.

What is this greater reality that gives one the purpose and meaning of life? The way to a greater purpose in life will be presented in this book. The way to know the purpose of one's own life will also be explained.

It is one thing to receive the truth from this book. It is another thing to incorporate and integrate that truth fully into one's life, one's mind, one's thinking, one's awareness and one's consciousness.

Behind every truth exists a greater truth. Beyond each learning lies a greater learning.

There is no end to learning. This is what the great learned thinkers throughout history have shown us.

There comes a time in many people's lives when they think or say, "Is this all there is to life?" or "There has to be more to life than what I am experiencing."

This type of questioning that comes from an inner urge to know the truth leads one to begin the journey toward Self mastery.

This highest truth is Universal Truth. Universal Truths apply to anyone, anywhere, and at anytime. Universal Truths exist universally. They explain creation and the functioning of the universe. Universal Truths explain the keys we need to come to know the Real Self.

There exists the self we experience through the five senses and the brain. There exists a Higher or High Self or Real Self we can only experience and come to know through the mind.

Mind is the vehicle Self uses or can use to come to know the Self. In other words, mind is the vehicle you can use to know who you are and the purpose of life. This being the case, since everyone has a mind, why doesn't everyone know the purpose of life? The answer is most people do not know how to discipline the mind and thereby bring it under the control of Self.

It has been said that a disciplined mind is your best friend. Yet very few people know this best friend because few people have a disciplined mind.

How does one gain a disciplined mind? The first and basic step is to practice a concentration exercise. Then as you begin to develop a more disciplined mind over a period of weeks or months, you may progress to meditation. Meditation is that special form of concentration used to listen to the inner Self by developing a still mind.

A still mind is absolutely essential to know the Self and to discover the purpose of life.

The reason a still mind is so very important is because thoughts get in the way of perceiving the true reality. Think about it. If your mind is busy thinking your old memory thoughts while another is speaking, you will not be able to fully receive what another is saying to you.

Undivided attention is necessary to receive the full benefit from any learning opportunity. Undivided attention means one's whole attention is on the person, place or thing.

Will power is an important factor in any success, yet without purpose a great understanding of will is often of little use.

The Universal purpose of life is to grow in awareness and understanding. Ultimately this growing awareness matures into wisdom and enlightenment.

Why do people fail to know the purpose of life? It is because they seek the temporary and miss the permanent and lasting.

The nature of physical life is change.

The nature of our physical world is change.

The nature of the physical universe is change.

The nature of the physical body is temporary.

The nature of the conscious mind is temporary.

The nature of sensory experience is temporary.

The nature of the five senses is temporary.

The nature of love is permanent and lasting.

The nature of truth is permanent and lasting.

The nature of Universal Laws are lasting.

The nature of Universal Principles are lasting.

The nature of the soul or subconscious mind is
     permanent.

The nature of the superconscious mind is lasting.

The nature of I AM is permanent and lasting.

The nature of understanding or understandings of Self is
     lasting.

The nature of understanding or understandings of creation is permanent.

The nature of understanding or understandings of Mind is permanent, lasting and eternal.

Two people can have the same experience at the same time and yet have totally different perceptions about that experience.

Why have some people become enlightened one, two, three or more thousand years ago and yet most people are still not enlightened in the present time period? In order to become enlightened one must find and learn the purpose of life. Then one must apply the Self to mastering this purpose. One must apply the Self and the mind until one's purpose unfolds and the Real Self achieves the full meaning of life.

How did these incredible beings become enlightened so far ahead of the rest of humanity?

The answer is,

They made different choices.

What are these different choices?

They are choices that enhance one's ability to know and understand what is lasting and real.

The reason the way to enlightenment seems so difficult to learn and understand is because we can't see it with the physical eyes, we can't smell it with the physical nose, we can't hear it with the physical ears, we can't taste it with the physical tongue and we can't touch it with the physical skin.

For many people the belief or assumption is, if I can't see it, taste it, hear it, smell it or touch it, then it doesn't exist. Nothing could be further from the truth.

Molecules aren't seen with the physical eyes yet they exist. Air isn't seen with the physical eyes yet every breath you take proves air exists. Atoms are not seen yet they exist.

In order to come to know the truth, purpose and meaning to life there must be the acceptance within the Self that there is a life and experience that is much more lasting, permanent and eternal than our temporary physical experiences.

The purpose of life has to be more than temporary, and it is. The purpose of life is lasting, permanent and eternal. Otherwise, what we do is a waste.

The five physical senses never give us the experience of what is permanent and lasting. They give us the experience of the temporary. The five senses give us the experience of the changes in weather, of the changes in our heartbeat, of the changes in scenery, of the changes in food, of the changes of the odors in the air, and of the changes in the sounds around us.

In short, in order to fulfill one's purpose there must be the realization that there is more to life than meets the eye.

People achieve greatness because they have great purposes. The conscious mind must be disciplined in order to be utilized fully and most efficiently.

Purpose is personal benefit.

Purpose begins with Self and includes Self. In order to know yourself you must do things for yourself. This is the admittance of one's Self value.

As you cause yourself to be a better person by practicing purpose in all you do you become much more capable of helping and aiding many more people.

By constantly practicing the discipline of having or creating purpose regularly, day by day you become a better and more fulfilled person. Day by day you discover more of the purpose of life and week by week you become aware of your purpose.

You can be very idealistic yet until there is purpose that idealism may not accomplish much. This is because until there is purpose you will lack the motivation required to succeed. People often fail to complete those goals and ideals that challenge them to change and go beyond limitation. This is because they lack the continual motivation that comes from purpose.

Ideals and activity are connected by purpose. Goals and action are connected by purpose. Dreams and effort are connected by purpose.

Stable, productive thoughts lead to stable, productive emotions. So purpose helps one build more stable and productive emotions. Many people would like to become more stable emotionally and purpose helps accomplish this.

In order to live a purposeful life one must practice and cause purpose in the thoughts, in the emotions, in the actions and in the life everyday.

A disciplined mind leads to a still mind and a still mind is necessary to know one's purpose in life

Through the still mind is the Real Self known.

Through the still mind is one's purpose known.

Throughout my life I have disciplined my mind and through this have developed a greater and greater stillness in my mind. As this greater stillness has developed I have received greater and greater awareness of my purpose in life.

Few people discipline their minds to achieve one-pointed concentration.

Fewer still use the disciplined, concentrated mind to visualize or image what they desire to occur in their lives.

Fewer still imagine what they want to become.

Fewer still apply the disciplined, concentrated mind to become enlightened.

Each person needs to integrate concentration into their consciousness.

Each person needs to integrate stilling the mind into their consciousness.

Meditation enables one to use the developed, concentrated mind to create a still mind within the Self.

If you have ever learned to ride a bicycle you know that it takes some practice to learn to balance yourself. Yet, with diligent practice, after a while you can learn to ride a bicycle very well.

So it is with a disciplined mind. A good way to begin to develop a disciplined mind is to practice concentration on the object of your choice for 10 minutes each day. Gradually or quickly your concentration ability will improve.

Remember, discipline of the mind is the ability to hold the attention where one has chosen for as long as one wants.

Progression in the discipline of the mind entails choosing to give more and more of one's attention to what is permanent and lasting.

As one ages, the tendency for the undisciplined mind is for more and more of the attention to go to sensory engrossment and memory images.

In order to master your mind the physical body must also be brought under one's control. Therefore, choose what you eat rather than eating habitually.

We have the ability to choose. There are always choices in life. Therefore, a big factor in learning about one's purpose in life is to learn to make better and better choices. Choices come from thoughts. So in order to make better choices, you must learn to be aware of all your thoughts. Often what people think are choices are merely unconscious re-actions to external stimuli or habitual memory thoughts.

In addition, learn from every experience in order to be a more productive individual.

Learn to receive the essence of the Universal Learning in each and every experience. Then be diligent in integrating through practice and application this learning into one's consciousness.

This is why concentration and mental discipline are so very vital to a quickening of one's enlightenment and understanding of the purpose of life.

Even if someone walked up to you on the street and told you the purpose of life it would not necessarily advance your consciousness. This rapid advancement only comes when one creates ways to apply and practice the universal truth one has received.

It is necessary to know the Universal Laws and Universal Truths.

One of the Universal Laws and Universal Truths will now be described.

1. The Universal Law of Cause and Effect. All the physical forms and shapes around us began as a thought. A car, a chair, a house, a ring and clothes all began as a thought.

1. Universal Truth = Thought is cause.

Your thoughts are the cause of your life. It is through your thoughts that you create your life to be the way it is. You make decisions that affect your life based on your thoughts.

Your destiny is not physical. The place to achieve your destiny is.

Each person has a physical life. Yet physical life is not the end all and meaning to life. Physical life is meant to be used to build greater awareness and understanding of one's self, one's mind and one's connectedness to all of the created universe.

So the key then is to:

Learn how to learn the learning that lasts forever and is eternal.

What is this learning? This is the learning of Self and creation.

What is meant by the word learning? To receive the higher truth into one's Self and being.

How does one learn how to learn of Self and creation?
First and foremost you must learn to harness the power of the mind. This is accomplished through mental discipline.

The primary exercise or practice to learn to use, direct and wield the mind is concentration.

The objects of concentration are many and varied. What they have in common is that they do not entertain the senses or the brain. For example, one might concentrate on the tip of one's index finger or a dot on the wall or an orange. The important point is the object should be still in order that the mind and the thought of the mind may be trained to be still.

Until one has learned to concentrate or focus the mind there will be little progress in controlling and directing the thoughts.

Until one learns to direct the thoughts there will be little progress in stilling the mind.

Until one learns to still the mind there will be little progress in aligning the conscious and subconscious minds in order to attune them to superconscious mind.

Until one has aligned conscious and subconscious minds there will be little ability to draw upon one's subconscious mind.

In order to know one's purpose in life one must draw upon knowledge and wisdom from one's soul or individual subconscious mind which resides in the great Universal Subconscious Mind.

It is your soul or individual subconscious mind existing in the great Universal Subconscious Mind between lifetimes and prior to each lifetime that calculates your need for learning and growth and thereby chooses your purpose for a lifetime.

In other words, you as a soul existing in Subconscious Mind choose your individual purpose for this lifetime before your birth in this incarnation. Yet you, existing in the brain and to some degree in the conscious mind have forgotten or lack awareness of the choice you made while in subconscious mind. This is because until the conscious mind is disciplined most people do not have controlled access to the knowledge and wisdom stored in their own subconscious mind.

The conscious mind of the individual must be trained and disciplined in order to be prepared to receive the knowledge, wisdom, purpose and assignment from one's subconscious mind. **To know your destiny you must have a disciplined conscious mind.**

Not only must the conscious mind be disciplined it must also be open to learning. **In other words, to know your purpose you must have an open mind.**

Thought to remember:
> You have a purpose in life.

What to do:
> Discover and fulfill your purpose.

Chapter 2
Your Purpose and the Still Mind

The still mind is necessary to know the purpose of life.

Most people who feel fulfilled in life have a focused or directed mind.

People who fulfill their purpose in life are able to concentrate and direct their thoughts to the goal, ideal and purpose desired. In directing their thoughts, their mind becomes quieter. As the mind quiets and stills, the inner purpose of one's Real Self is able to be received in the conscious mind.

One's purpose in life does not come from the physical brain. It doesn't even come from one's conscious mind, which is one's consciousness inhabiting the brain.

One's purpose in life comes from one's subconscious or inner mind which is something called the soul. I find the term subconscious mind to be more scientific and understandable.

The conscious mind and brain must be caused to be receptive. They are not normally so. In an undisciplined state, the conscious mind is full of thoughts as it responds or re-acts to the constant stimuli entering the brain through the five senses of sight, smell, taste, touch and sound.

In order to be receptive one needs to focus the mind enough on what one desires in order to receive. This focusing and directing of the attention causes the mind for a time to become more still. It is in this stillness that one receives the inner guidance necessary to fulfill life's mission.

People that fulfill life's purpose are able to tap into that inner guidance. Then they are able to create and find ways to manifest, create, or achieve that inner message of guidance in the outer, waking, physical world.

It is instruction that comes from deep within our own being.

A still and receptive mind is necessary to be able to trust oneself and others. A still mind will allow you to receive the manifestation of your desires. Too often people miss out on opportunities that present themselves in life because the mind is too busy with other thoughts.

A still mind will allow one to trust in the working of the Universal Laws.

A still mind will allow one to listen to others so one will know what and when to give.

A still mind will allow one to trust the unlimited truth and wisdom that is within the Self.

A still mind will enable one to be in the present moment, thereby, valuing the present experience.

A still mind will enable one to have a greater sense of purpose. One will, in fact, receive and know a greater purpose.

A still mind will enable one to trust the choices one makes that are in alignment with who one wants to be and become.

Ways to Develop a Still Mind

1. Observe the breath.

Give your full attention to the in-breath and the out-breath and the time or space between breaths. Think of nothing else. In fact, do not think at all. Just observe the breath.

When I was a child I found it very annoying at times that I could not seem to stop watching or observing my breath, my breathing. I wanted to have my attention on my play and my exploration of nature.

Now I know the great value of this understanding of breath that I inherently possessed as a child.

The breath is the most important factor for keeping the physical body alive. It is the breath that binds the Real or Inner Self to the body. Therefore, it is of prime importance that each individual learn to observe and use the breath for the upliftment of one's consciousness and the fulfillment of life's purpose.

2. Give full attention to others.

Caring for others, loving others, and service to others all function as a valuable point of focus and thereby aid in stilling the mind.

When giving to others the mind can be present in the now. It is only in the now, the present moment, that one can fulfill the next step of one's life purpose. By being fully present with one's thoughts, mind and attention one can assimilate the essence of the permanent learning available in the present experience.

3. Affirm that the present moment is very important and therefore worth giving your full attention.

Memory is very valuable. Memory allows us to recall situations, circumstances, and events in the past that have a bearing on the present.

Imagination is also very valuable. When used correctly imagination enables us to visualize or image the direction we wish the mind to move toward. By imagining our future we are more likely to create the future the way we desire, for the mind is meant to be the servant of you, the individual.

However, the mind is not meant to be kept busy all the

time remembering the past or visualizing-imaging the future.

There comes a time when it is necessary to rest the mind. This needs to be done every day. Every day there needs to be some time spent thinking and some time spent not thinking.

Why is time spent not thinking important? Because the time given to a still mind is the present time available for the wise, knowledge-filled subconscious mind to give to the less mature, conscious mind.

Only when you are not thinking thoughts are you capable of receiving the thoughts of another. To listen is to receive the thoughts of another. To receive the thoughts of another requires that you do not think thoughts of your own while the other person is speaking.

In a like manner, in order to receive the guidance, wisdom and power of the subconscious mind one must be still, mentally, and listen.

4. Meditate every day.

Meditation is the quality of stilling the mind in order to receive.

One can meditate in order to receive the high knowledge from one's subconscious mind.

One can meditate in order to align conscious and subconscious minds and attune them to superconscious mind.

One can meditate in order to know God.

One can meditate to gain enlightenment.

One can meditate to relieve stress.

One can meditate to find and know peace.

One can meditate to open the Self to love.

On can meditate in order to receive one's purpose for life.

One can meditate in order to make life more fulfilling.

One can meditate to know Self.

5. Practice a concentration exercise every day.

Practice of concentration precedes a still mind. Until concentration is practiced, many of the thoughts of the Self are not even known. The person remains unconscious or unaware of many of the thoughts.

One day, a few months after I had begun the daily practice of concentrating on a candle flame, I drove up to a stop light. The street light was red so I stopped. While waiting for the light to change to green my attention and mind wandered. One thought led to another and soon I was thinking my fifth associated memory thought. All of a sudden I realized this and I said, "This is not what I want to think about. I want all my attention to be on the street light!" Immediately all my attention was drawn back to the red street light and there it remained until the light turned green.

As the light turned green I drove away with a sense of exhilaration and power I had never before experienced. It was the thrill and power of being aware of what my undisciplined mind was doing and having the awareness to make a choice to direct my attention and still my mind.

Because thought is cause, thought is the beginning and essence of all power. The person who learns to choose their own thoughts and masters their own thoughts has power to gain enlightenment and fulfill the purpose of a lifetime.

The mind is the vehicle the Self uses to know Self and creation. Thought is the tool the mind uses to create.

In order to really know and fulfill your purpose in life you are going to have to practice a concentration exercise every day. After one or more months of this you will need to add meditation. This is because meditation is that special form of concentration utilized for the purpose of knowing the Self.

In concentration one learns to focus and direct the

thoughts, then become aware of the thoughts, then know the thoughts, then choose the thoughts. All of these are necessary in order to know and fulfill one's life purpose.

6. Choose a time period each day to think no thoughts.

Throughout the day each person needs to concentrate on having a still mind. A still mind means having no thoughts in one's head. This means you are not thinking. Each person each day needs to spend some time in not thinking.

To some people the idea of not thinking might seem ridiculous or inconceivable. Some people think they are their thoughts. This is untrue. You are not your thoughts. However, you do become as you think.

When you think no thoughts the mind is still. When the mind is still you are peaceful, quiet, and fulfilled. When the mind is stilled you can experience who you really are, the Real Self.

When you constantly think, you come to believe that you are your thoughts, which is untrue.

When the mind is still you have the ability to choose a thought with conscious awareness and thereby realize you are not the thought.

By choosing as your initiation point, a still mind, the power to choose a thought is realized. By realizing the power to choose a thought one realizes the power to create for thought is the cause of all creation. The causal thought is created by an individual.

The more one masters a still mind the more one knows creation.

The more one masters a still mind the more one understands one's ability to create.

The more one masters a still mind the more one knows purpose.

Purpose is achieved by one who knows the thoughts of Self and chooses them.

In order to know the purpose of life and your purpose in life you must develop a still mind.

A still mind can receive a thought from another person or from your inner Self.

Your purpose in life is determined by your subconscious mind.

Therefore, you need to have a still mind in order to consciously receive and be aware of the purpose your subconscious mind has already given you.

The undisciplined conscious mind does not know or remember the purpose given from subconscious mind. Only the disciplined, still conscious mind can remember and receive this mission or assignment of a lifetime.

Great inventions are not made by thinking hard. Rather they come when the outer conscious mind is stilled and can then receive from the inner subconscious or superconscious mind.

7. Vow that receiving the essence of the learning in every situation, every experience, in the present is more important than being right or wrong.

Too often people fail to learn and grow because they become entrenched in their ego identification with old thoughts, old ideas, old theories from the past that no longer hold true in the present. Living in old memories will keep you from learning in the present experience.

The correct use of memory is to aid the individual to perform tasks more efficiently, productively and easily in the present.

Most people dwell way too much on the past. Attachments to the past are formed. Examples are angers about past hurts, grudges about past hurts, hatreds about perceived past hurts, resentments, condemnation and guilt about the past.

One may also be attached to the good times about the past. A person may think the past is better than the present and pine for the good old days that will never return.

As long as a person dwells in the past that person can never get the full benefit from the present. **More specifically, the degree to which one dwells in the past is the degree to which one is ineffective in the present.**

The present is where the learning exists. The present is where you will find your purpose. Therefore, cause yourself to be open to the learning in each experience. **Ask yourself, what is the essence of the learning in each experience.**

Strive to have most of your attention in the present. Give in the present and receive in the present.

Image, visualize or imagine your goal or ideal and then place your attention in the present in order to fulfill that goal or ideal.

A goal is what you want to do.
An ideal is what you want to be.
A goal is what you want to achieve.
An ideal is what you want to become.

The only time to achieve is in the present.
The only time to receive is in the present.
The only time to do is in the present.
The only time to become is in the present.

Now, the present, is the time, the only time there is.

Purpose gives you personal benefit for what you are doing right now.

When you create a purpose you are creating a desire from
within, rather than waiting for an outside physical stimulus. The
outer environment stimulates desires all the time. For example,
advertising intends to stimulate a desire to buy a product.

As you become more conscious and awake to the real
meaning of life your choice and decisions evolve also. The decisions become less based upon temporary ego and sensory gratification and more based upon permanent and lasting fulfillment
and the growth of the Whole Self.

Purpose gives one the ability to complete what one begins. When people fail it is usually at the ending or completion
stage.

Purpose provides the inner desire and motivation to complete or finish what you begin.

8. Give gratitude for every experience in life. Give gratitude for
the experiences of the past. Find a reason for giving gratitude
and being grateful for any person you hold a grudge against.

Giving gratitude releases the giver from the restrictions
and limitations of the past.

Until you can find something to be grateful for concerning past hurts, you will not release your attachment to the hurt
from the past. Therefore, you are trapped in the past.

Gratitude must be stated out loud. It is not enough just to
think it. It must be stated out loud at least once a day for 100
days. It may seem to hurt when you first give gratitude because
of the previous resistance, yet the pain will soon fade into freedom and peace.

Why does gratitude work? Gratitude helps the individual
practicing it because it updates and upgrades one's whole sys-

tem, mentally, emotionally, and physically by bringing you into the present while aligning you with Universal Truth and Universal Laws.

Gratitude brings you into the present.

Anger, increasing fear, hatred, condemnation and guilt are all of the past. They are based upon past ways of thinking and unresolved hurts. They are not based in the highest reasoning.

Gratitude gives the one practicing it a way to resolve the past and let it go. Gratitude helps to release old, emotional attachments.

By looking to discover at least one aspect of an experience that benefitted you in any way, you can change your perspective. You can change your perspective from anger to gratitude. The perspective changes from all that was lost to something, no matter how small, that was gained. Perhaps you learned a valuable lesson.

For example, you might say:

I am grateful for (insert name of person). Say this out loud every day until you really mean it and can feel it. One hundred times a day is even better. Once you can really feel the gratitude and experience it as an honest gratitude then the past attachments to hate, anger, fear, guilt, etc. will be released. The thoughts will be replaced and upgraded to higher thoughts of compassion, thus giving you freedom from the past. You will exist more fully in the present as a creative, successful being.

Purpose is very, very powerful. Never underestimate it. It can give you the motivation to accomplish anything.

If you are not motivated to do something, you won't do it unless you have an outside factor to motivate you, or you can create purpose. Therefore, purpose is of utmost importance for anyone who desires to have continual motivation to achieve anything ranging from a pay raise to enlightenment.

The urge for enlightenment, for a fulfilling life, to achieve one's purpose in life, must come from within.

The more you create purpose and live by it, the more you will be tied into the inner urge. Your conscious mind will become aligned with your subconscious mind. Your conscious mind will then receive the wisdom your subconscious mind offers. That is the power of purpose. Purpose is very powerful. Never underestimate it.

Physically-minded people tend to think in terms of physical goals.

Mentally and spiritually evolved people tend to also think in terms of ideals. Yet they still have goals. This is because every time you advance your consciousness, every time you learn and grow you don't lose anything, although one may choose to release past limitations.

To grow from adolescence into adulthood does not require you lose something. Instead you add to the learning, experience, and knowledge that are already yours, while at the same time letting go of what is no longer needed.

When you want to possess something you have a desire.

When you want to be or become something you have an ideal.

As each great learning is completed, be willing and motivated to do whatever is necessary to advance to the next stage of awareness and fulfillment. New choices and opportunities will present themselves.

At these times of change and movement into the next stage of life it is important to remember to continually create purpose for the initiation of the next cycle.

Nothing physical is lasting. All physical things change, wear away or deteriorate. What does last is the truth we learn and the love we give, share and receive.

Desires can come from an environmental stimulus or they

can be caused inwardly from purpose. These caused desires, when pursued, evolve into higher desires that then evolve into the real needs of the inner self. The real needs are to know the truth, to gain the high wisdom and enlightenment, and to receive and give the deeper, all-encompassing love.

The desire that proceeds from an environmental stimulus is of the senses and physical brain.

The desire that comes from purpose and is therefore caused by the individual is of the mind. It affords the opportunity for greater self understanding and self awareness.

When one finally tires of sensory gratification and stimulation one goes looking for the higher knowledge.

I once gave a student the following affirmation to say several times each day: <u>Purpose is personal benefit. Purpose starts with me and includes me. I must do things for myself in order to know myself</u>.

After practicing this affirmation every day for one month my student said, "I feel like a completely different person. It is one of the biggest and most dramatic changes I have ever experienced in my life." It's like the difference between night and day.

In order to know the big purpose of life it is necessary to create and practice purpose in the little things done and accomplished each day. State your purpose, out loud, each day, over and over again until the idea is fixed not only in the conscious mind but also the brain.

When the conscious mind is disciplined and directed then it becomes receptive to the inner urge from the subconscious mind.

Teaching others the truth you have found in life is also productive in drawing your purpose out from your inner self, your subconscious mind. When you teach, truth seems to flow out from within you. Often you will not even be aware you had this truth within yourself. This truth connects with the higher purpose and fulfillment is experienced.

To choose a purpose requires will. Every time you choose a thought, that thought becomes stronger. To choose a purpose is a specific kind of thought. To continually choose or create a purpose is to build a strong thought of purpose.

Practice the little purposes every day in order to build to knowing the big purpose of life.

Purpose is found in the still mind.

The challenge in life is to continually refine and improve your thoughts. This is because we determine our life with our thoughts. The choices we make are based upon our thoughts.

If one thinks unproductive thoughts one will make unproductive choices and decisions. If one thinks productive thoughts one will make productive thoughts and decisions.

If one spends some of one's time in a receptive state of no thought one will receptively draw to the Self much of what one needs to fulfill the Self. This requires mental discipline.

There are two main factors or principles of creation. They are the aggressive and receptive principles. Receptivity has a drawing power and is best created from a still mind. The aggressive principle has the initiating power within it and is also best initiated from a still mind.

It would seem then that the ability to create a still mind is one's best opportunity to be productive, to create and fulfill one's purpose in life.

It is truth that a disciplined mind is needed to fully understand and fulfill one's purpose in life. It is also truth that a disciplined mind is necessary to produce a still mind.

Why is a disciplined mind necessary to fulfill one's purpose in life? **A disciplined mind can produce a still mind in a**

thought-free state. A still mind has no conscious mind thought. This thought-free, still conscious mind then provides space for thoughts or instruction about one's purpose. This purpose comes from one's subconscious mind into one's conscious awareness.

A still conscious mind can receive the higher truth, wisdom and awareness from the subconscious mind and even from the superconscious mind.

This is why a disciplined conscious mind is so very important and vital to achieving one's purpose in life.

Thought to remember:
The mind is the vehicle of the Real Self.

What to do:
Discipline your mind.

Chapter 3
Ideals, Goals and Purpose

The life we lead is made up of images. These images may be physical images we see with our eyes or mental images we create in our minds. These mental images can also be called mental pictures. Visualization is basically directing the creation of mental images in the mind.

A thought is a mental image. Everything created began as a thought. An idea is a thought image that you find useful. Each person has many thoughts each day. Those thoughts that seem useful enough to get one's attention are useful ideas.

The world is filled with ideas, from the clothes you wear to the house where you live. Someone had the thought of creating a building or owning a clothing factory. Even if your clothes are homemade, someone still had the idea of making them. Someone designed, planned and constructed the house you live in and this requires thoughts, ideas and mental images.

I am going to present you with an idea that is universal. That idea is <u>Thought is Cause</u>. What does this statement, "thought is cause," mean or indicate? Thought is cause means that everything begins with a thought. Therefore, thought is the point of power. Thought is the point of control.

In order to bring about or manifest a thought in your life you must learn to mentally picture, image, or imagine what you desire to create in your life. A thought or idea is the beginning of any creation. Successful people always have an image or idea that they hold in mind constantly. This image or thought revolves around the success they desire to create or manifest in their life.

Thought is the beginning of all physical effects we experience in our life.

Success includes whatever you have imaged and then achieved that was good and productive. Success could be measured according to physical wealth accumulated. It could be measured according to a loving family and friends. It could be measured according to degrees of enlightenment. In other words, success can be measured in many different ways.

I find the following question to be of value in assessing the success of any endeavor. Does it benefit the Self _and_ other people? True and great success always involves helping other people.

Thought is the beginning of all the physical effects we experience in our lives. It has been said that nothing is more powerful than an idea whose time has come.

An example of an idea whose time had come was the founding of the United States of America. At the time the idea of a country governing itself through elected rulers and without a king was radical. Over 200 years later that idea has been accepted and practiced by many countries around the world.

One time I had a student ask me, "What is the most powerful force in the universe?" To which I replied, "Thought is the most powerful force in the universe." Then the student said, "I think love is the most powerful thing in the universe." My response was, "Love is a thought." Love is a thought of connectedness in LIGHT.

You see, the essence of our being is LIGHT. We are individualized units of LIGHT known as I AM or plural I AM'S.

Therefore, our tool for creating is LIGHT. How do we form, shape and manifest LIGHT into our lives in the manner desired? The answer is thought. Thought is our vehicle for using LIGHT for the fulfillment of desires and needs. The key to using thought and therefore LIGHT, is to have a disciplined and focused mind that consistently and repeatedly images the thoughtform one desires to create in the life.

Goals are mental images or directed thoughts of what one wants to create outwardly in the life. Goals relate to physical things, objects, and situations in one's life.

One can have a goal of having more money. One can have a goal to complete some project.

Everyone needs goals for goals give direction to the mind.

What is the mind?

The mind is the vehicle of Self or I AM.

The Self uses the vehicle of the mind in order to progress in awareness and understanding.

The beginning of all creation is LIGHT. There are two main factors that come from LIGHT. These two factors are Truth and Love.

Truth is the Aggressive Principle of LIGHT.

Love is the Receptive Principle of LIGHT.

In order to progress in awareness one must learn to wield both of these.

What is an atom made of? We are told that an atom is made of protons, neutrons and electrons. Yet protons, neutrons and electrons are tiny compared to the space between the nucleus of an atom and the distance to its orbiting electrons. So an atom is mostly space. This space in the atom is not empty space for it is filled with energy.

We determine how this space in atoms is to be used by our thoughts. This is one of the lessons of Quantum mechanics. The experimenter affects the experiments with his or her thoughts.

You have gotten to the place, situations, and circumstances you are now living in as a result of your thoughts.

Decisions are based on thoughts. People make decisions

based upon thoughts they hold in their mind. Your decisions which are based upon your thoughts brought you to this place and circumstance in your life. Therefore the person that chooses the thoughts wisely and directs the mind with goals is much more likely to create success in the life.

Therefore, write down on paper your most important goals you would like to achieve. Visualize or image these goals until they have been achieved.

Remember, a goal gives direction to the mind and the mind is very powerful. In fact,

The mind is the tool or vehicle for knowing the Self.

The mind is your vehicle for creating your life.

Each person has a mind. Yet some people use their minds better than other people.

Choose any measure of success and you will find that those people that succeed use their minds more effectively than those that fail.

There are varying degrees of using the mind just as there are varying degrees of success and failure.

Until the mind is focused in a certain direction the attention and efforts of the individual will be scattered.

The basis of all thought is mental or mind images. For example, before you say the word "tree", you must first think of the picture of a tree.

Successful people understand that their thoughts are powerful and that thoughts are things. It is through our thoughts that we build up our world.

Directing our thoughts with goals gives each person a greater opportunity to create the life that he or she finds fulfilling. So therefore it is important to direct the mind every day upon certain predetermined lines of thought called goals.

Imagination is used to create goals. A goal by its very nature is something you have yet to achieve. Therefore, a goal is something of the future.

Memory uses images of the past.
Attention receives images in the present.
Imagination creates images for the future.

Goals are mainly physical. So when you think of a goal, you are thinking of something you want to achieve in the future. How soon will this goal of the future arrive? It depends in large part on the precision and strength of your mental image.

Refining your Goals

When going from the first floor to the second floor of a house a person goes up stair steps. Each step up gets the individual closer to the goal of being on the second floor.

In a similar manner often we have smaller goals that are steps on the way to great or larger goals.

With each step up the ladder or stairs it is important to learn the lessons the present situation offers.

The lesson may be confidence. The lesson may be self value. The lesson may be determination, discipline, love, communication, friendship, or other qualities that make for a better person.

In other words, because you want to achieve greater things then you must change, adapt, adjust and transform your consciousness.

ALL great achievements began as a thought. Therefore you need to do whatever is needed in order to learn to think greater thoughts and believe in the possibility of you achieving them.

The truth will set you free of limitations.

Therefore a very important and powerful key in manifesting goals is to be willing to receive new or greater truth into the Self. In other words, you need to learn the lesson that life is offering.

History is full of examples of people who at first did not succeed yet through perseverance and learning were able to achieve their greatest imaginings.

When things are not working out for you, change yourself. In order to change one must be willing to receive a greater truth into the Self.

We learn through our five senses of sight, smell, taste, touch and hearing. Therefore it is very important to remain open to the learning in one's experiences.

If you are not achieving your goals as fast as you desire then it is time to look at yourself and life from a different perspective. This requires receiving a greater truth into yourself.

Some people are afraid to change because they think that this will mean they were wrong up to the present time. Such a person thinks, "If I admit I was wrong up to now then my life must have little meaning." This is wrong thinking.

To learn in the present does not negate the past. Instead, learning in the present indicates one has added to his or her ability to succeed in the present and in the future.

Desires are what you want to receive.
Goals are what you want to achieve.
Desires have the power to draw to you what is desired.
Goals aid you to move toward your imaged objective.
Both function from a mental image.

Once a person tastes success then the appetite is whetted for more success. Success breeds success because success is an attitude. The attitude that leads to success is a clearly imaged goal that he frequently holds in the mind's eye until it is achieved.

An attitude is a thought or group of thoughts held in the mind and practiced until it becomes second nature.

An attitude is a repeated collection of thoughts.

Thoughts can be either productive or unproductive. So if one is going to practice a thought it is reasonable to focus on thoughts that are productive-thoughts that when created or manifested will bring permanent and lasting fulfillment.

Everyone is dependent upon the environment to receive new thoughts and new ideas about life. A child learns and grows by receiving knowledge, ideas and experience into the Self. Childhood is a time of rapid learning. Therefore, remember to stay open to learning at all times.

Keep an open mind.

When creating a goal the mind moves aggressively to form an image of what one intends to create or do.

When one stills the mind and has an open mind one can receive the learning, knowledge, information and experience one needs in order to be capable of receiving the goal.

To have or believe in a new and greater goal or your next step requires greater thinking. It requires a belief in the possibility that you can be greater.

ALL minds think in pictures. Therefore, mental images or pictures are not only the key but also the power of using the mind. Mind is the vehicle the Self uses to create. Therefore, use the mind to create success. **Mind is the vehicle the Self uses to create.**

To set a goal or create a goal and to be committed to achieving that goal can be perceived as a risk. After all, aren't you comfortable being the way you are now? You do seem to be able to survive with your life as it is now. However, is that all you want out of life? Do you want more than survival? More than the fight or flight of an animal? Of course you do. So therefore, become a risk taker.

The greatest risk is to do nothing!
    The challenge to any person who wants to succeed in life is to continually refine, upgrade and improve one's thoughts. Thought is cause. Therefore, we create our world around us based upon our thoughts.

Continually refine, upgrade and improve your thoughts.

    When shooting arrows with a bow, always keep your attention on the target. The target is your goal. The goal is to shoot the arrow so that the arrow hits the target in the very center.
    So it is with any goal in life. Keep your attention on the goal. Then, like the arrow, move or fly straight to the goal. Use whatever tool is needed to image the goal clearly and to hold it in mind.
    1. Repeat the goal outloud every day.
    2. Write the goal on paper and read it every day.
    3. Share your goal with others that will be receptive to it.
    In short, continually upgrade and improve the image of the goal.
    It has been said, "What the mind can conceive, it can achieve."

This is true because all creations begin as a thought.
    Remember, the first two letters of the word GOAL spells

GO

The second two letters are AL. Who is AL? AL is you! AL is the creator within you. AL is your ability to learn and grow as you

<u>GO</u> or move toward your imaged mental construct.

If you will think about it, consider that all your education up to the present time has occurred through the medium of pictures. To see a person or object through sight is to view a 2 dimensional or 3 dimensional image or picture.

Sounds received through the sense of hearing give us a type or kind of image or impression as does touch, smell, and taste.

A mental image or picture then is the way experiences structure themselves as they are received into one's mind.

ALL the ancient languages were written in pictures by people who understood the picture language. The picture written languages are called hieroglyphs, or petroglyphs or pictoglyphs. Before the invention or coming of the alphabet, written languages were inscribed by using groups of pictures. Each picture had a specific meaning. Even to this day the Chinese do not use an alphabet and instead have many symbols that were originally pictures. Each picture represents an idea or word.

Your night dreams come in the form of pictures. Your day dreams come in the form of pictures.

Since the mind is alway working in pictures it makes sense that we would use the mind most effectively by choosing and directing these pictures or images of the mind.

The truth is people create mental images every day. So choose the mental images you want to achieve. This is called setting a goal or creating a goal.

The only way you will achieve is to have a mental image or goal of what you want to achieve.

Before you entered this lifetime you chose a mental image of your upcoming life, and you have attempted to fulfill this ever since.

So you see we always have a choice as to the thoughts we think.

If you want to change the world then you must change yourself. To change yourself means to permanently alter the way you think by thinking different thoughts that are more in alignment with Universal Law and Universal Truth.

Once you raise your level of awareness you will look back upon the past and wonder, "How could I have ever thought like that?" You may think "There sure were a lot of things that I didn't see and perceive then that I do now", or "I wish I had known then what I know now."

The point is, "You can raise your level of awareness by stilling your mind."

By the still mind is the real self known.

The one who would be free must create greater thought in the present.

A goal gives the mind direction. It focuses the mind on what you want to do in order to achieve. A goal is usually something physical that you want to achieve.

For example, you may have a goal to drive a car or chop wood or to sweep the floor. Therefore, this mental image or goal is pictured or visualized in the mind or the mind's eye. The most efficient way to use the mind is to direct it. A goal clearly imaged gives direction to the mind.

A strong purpose helps to keep a goal from getting too fixed and inflexible. A purpose or personal benefit allows the goal to evolve as we learn, grow and evolve.

A mental picture is a thought. Words are a physical manifestation of a thought, a type of activity.

The difference between goals and desires is that a goal provides a mental image for the individual to move towards.

A desire provides a mental image for the subconscious mind to fulfill.

A tool that aids in manifesting desires is the ten most

wanted list. The word manifest means to bring a thought into physical existence.

A ten most wanted list is a way of ordering one's thoughts using proper perspective. This is accomplished by placing one's most wanted, most important or greatest desire at the top of the list. In the number two spot goes one's second most important desire. Number three on your ten most wanted list is your third greatest desire. Continue this process until ten items are placed on the ten most wanted list. For example, a new car may be number one on the ten most wanted list. A new job may be number two. A new pair of shoes may be number three and so on. Read the ten most wanted list each day in order to prioritize your thoughts.

Reading the ten most wanted list each day has a dual function. The first is to aid the conscious mind to focus in on what is important in the life. In this way the energies of the day are better spent by focusing on what is important in the life.

The second function of the ten most wanted list is that it enables one's conscious mind to give clear images to one's subconscious mind. The subconscious mind is very powerful and will go to work or move to fulfill the desire images of the conscious mind. So by creating a ten most wanted list and reading it every day one engages the conscious and subconscious minds in harmony. This is very powerful. In addition, if one's subconscious mind is unable to fulfill the conscious mind's clearly imaged desire then the subconscious mind will reach out to other subconscious minds to connect with them in the fulfillment of one's desires.

For example, that seemingly chance meeting with a person that introduces you to another person that provides you with the job or resources you need is not an accident at all. That experience was provided by subconscious mind. This is why desires are something you receive whereas goals are something you achieve.

The world is full of sensory stimulus. Yet sensory stimulus alone will never give success. Physical experience alone will never give enlightenment. It is what you <u>do</u> with the physical experience that determines your rate of soul growth and spiritual development.

Sensory experience is to be used to glean universal truth, the essence of the soul learning in each experience.

Most everyone loves sensory experiences such as tasty food, beautiful scenery, wonderful smells, etc.

Stimulus leads to desires and the most basic desires are physical. It is each person's duty to evolve physical desires to mental desires. Mental desires are of the mind. The mind is our vehicle for knowing the Self. Therefore, it is important that we learn to think with and use the mind.

When a person lives for sensory stimulus then that person's consciousness resides in the physical brain. Such a person does not have the opportunity or availability of the use of the mind. The mind is much more powerful and expansive than the brain. Yet the brain must be used correctly in order to then use the mind to build permanent understandings of Self and Creation.

The desires that come from physical stimulus are temporary. So the solution is to gain desires in a different way. The solution, the way out of this dilemma, is to create and fulfill desires in a different more evolved and uplifting way. This more evolved, uplifting and different way is called purpose.

What is purpose?

Purpose is personal benefit. Purpose can be and usually is self created. Purpose aligns with goals because purpose provides the motivation to pursue a goal.

Think about it. When does a goal become really attractive to you? A goal becomes attractive or desirable when there is a benefit to you, the goal creator. Purpose provides an inner source of desire and an inner source of motivation because purpose is personal benefit.

Since you created the purpose for a goal, that purpose and that motivation and that desire can last as long as you choose to maintain or have that purpose. Outer stimulus is always temporary. In contrast, the inner motivation to achieve that comes from purpose can be lasting and permanent.

You the individual choose the thoughts that are lasting and eternal or temporary and changing. That is a great key of the deepening, enlightened life. By choosing thoughts that are permanent and lasting you connect with Universal Truth. For anything to be lasting and eternal it must connect with Universal Truth.

Therefore, when you create a purpose you can cause lasting desire for motivation.

Examine your thoughts. Do you want to wait for a stimulus to come to you in order to create a desire? Do you <u>want</u> to wait on the environment to provide this or would you rather be able and capable of creating purposeful motivation to achieve desires every day?

Sometimes companies bring in a paid motivational speaker. That speaker gets all the employees excited. From this excitement the employees produce to greater degrees. Yet after a few weeks or a few months this excitement wears off because the employees have not developed a greater purpose.

So purpose, which is personal benefit, needs to be interiorized.

As the individual evolves so does one's purpose evolve. This evolving purpose involves and includes more and more people. The greatest purpose or personal benefit lies in aiding other people in their soul growth because connectedness is the true nature of reality. Therefore, as you aid others to abundance you are also aided to abundance.

As one expands the consciousness to include others, the benefit returned to the self becomes greater and greater.

The more you practice purpose the more your purpose continues to elevate. The solution is to always strive to elevate your thoughts. Mental discipline is required in order to continually upgrade one's purpose and the ability to give and receive.

It requires discipline to think a different thought. To choose a different thought is to use your mind. To think the same thought day after day is to be in the brain. A person can either choose thought with the mind or repeat memory thoughts from the brain.

Ideals concern all the productive, valuable and good things one can become. Ideals involve achieving more of your full potential.

Examples of ideals are to become full of love, filled with truth, knowing, wisdom or compassion.

The greatest ideal is enlightenment. At the essence and core of our being is LIGHT. At the essence of every atom in our physical body is LIGHT. Each individual is an I AM, an individualized unit of LIGHT. It is each soul's duty, each person's duty to know self as a creator. A creator is made up of the LIGHT of awareness and uses LIGHT to create.

Mind is the vehicle I AM uses in order to create. Mind is the vehicle I AM uses to learn to be a creator. And mind is made up of LIGHT also. Each level and each division of mind uses LIGHT at varying rates of vibration.

It is good and productive to give people hope and inspire them to be more and be greater than they are already.

It is productive for a teacher to say to a student, "I can see or perceive you becoming great" or "I can perceive you becoming a spiritual teacher" or "I can see what you have to offer has lasting value." A teacher may say to the student, "I can see you becoming a world teacher or I believe you can become a great healer."

There are many wonderful thoughts and ideas that a

teacher can say to a student that stimulate a huge belief that he or she can become much greater and achieve great and wonderful needs for self and humanity.

It has been said that there is nothing more powerful than an idea whose time has come. This is a very true statement because thought is cause. In other words everything begins with a thought.

Love fills the universe and is at its essence. Love together with truth give each person the possibility and probability of evolving to know self and be enlightened.

In order to use goals and ideals most effectively one must learn to create clear and precise mental images. Each success in life was preceded by a mental image, a thought that was mentally pictured over and over again in the mind's eye.

In order to create greater thoughts there must be the acceptance that the present life one is experiencing is not satisfying or not fully satisfying. Then because of one's self value and worth, a greater or improved image of self and the life can be created.

The way out of an unfulfilling life is to first imagine something greater. Goals and ideals are those imaged thoughts that we create a greater life around.

In order to progress to a better life each individual needs to receive a higher truth.

You have to and need to receive a higher truth through the five senses of sight, smell, taste, touch and hearing. This is the way learning is accomplished in a physical body and in the brain. This is the way we build permanent understandings of self in physical life.

As the higher truth is received it needs to be integrated into one's thinking and one's consciousness.

Ask yourself the following question:
"How will my thoughts improve?" and "What limiting

thoughts am I going to replace with more expansive thoughts?"

Another question to ask yourself is, "What false or partially wrong thoughts will I replace with right and productive thinking?"

Practicing mental discipline, such as concentration and meditation, aids and enables one to more easily identify one's thought. From these practices one can come to have 10 times more awareness in identifying one's thoughts.

How can you change your thoughts if you are not even aware of your thoughts? This is why so many people have difficulty changing. It is a truth that, "as you think so you become." Therefore, in order to become greater each person must think greater thoughts. In order to facilitate the process of thinking greater thoughts it certainly helps to be aware of one's thoughts.

If the thoughts in one's mind are racing then one can never hope to be fully aware of the thoughts. When the thoughts and the mind race, it is like a cart leading the horse or a cat chasing its tail. In both cases things are turned backwards. The Real Self, that is you, is supposed to lead the mind and direct the thoughts.

The challenge is to continually refine and improve one's thoughts. The need for the conscious mind is to be disciplined. Discipline of the conscious mind is required in order for Self to be capable of continually refining the thoughts. Stated another way, you have to be aware of your thoughts before you can consciously refine your thoughts.

Most people think 80 to 90% the same thoughts every day. This leaves 10 to 20% of the thoughts that go beyond memory and that can be employed with the imagination to improve one's mind and consciousness.

So a secret key of the mind is to learn to create new and greater thoughts each day and to come to rely less and less on

old memory thoughts every day.

This is just the opposite of what most people do. Most people when they are young start out thinking many new thoughts. As people age they end up thinking more and more repeated memory thoughts. Memory thoughts are images of the past, and people cannot learn and grow in the past. When one tries to live in the past one gets old and ages.

Therefore, it is wise to look upon each day as a new learning, a new experience, a new day to learn, change and grow.

New mental images in the conscious mind lead to new and different emotions that then lead to new activity, action or effort. Emotions connect thought pictures or images to activity. The written and spoken word is a kind of activity. So choosing new, productive, and creative thoughts leads to a greater and more open use of the emotions. This translates into more free-flowing writing and speaking abilities.

People that have writer's block find that when they change their thoughts in a new or different way, new ideas and words flow out of them and onto paper. They become better writers, better public speakers and more effective communicators. Their mental thoughts flow through the emotions and into the physical life.

Emotions are the glue that bind the conscious outer mind with the subconscious or inner mind. Emotions connect thought pictures with words.

A mind image or picture is mental. A spoken word is a physical abstraction. A written word is a physical abstraction.

A still mind aligns all three, of mental, emotional and physical.

There is a greater Self or a Higher Self that one can serve. By accepting the truth that you are more than a physical body there can begin to be the dawning of awareness of what you really are.

What is your ideal of yourself? Is the ideal of yourself the same as what is in your memory of yourself 10 years ago or is your ideal of yourself something that you are becoming?

Each person is in the process of becoming a greater individual. We can quicken this process of reaching our full potential or we can try to remain the same. The longer one refuses to learn the universal lessons of life the more painful the results of those choices become.

Discipline of the mind is necessary to know one's purpose in life. Even if someone were to tell you your purpose in life you still would not know your purpose in life. You might at that point believe you know your purpose in life or have information about your purpose in life. It would still be up to you, as an individual, to come to know your purpose in life by practicing and applying the information given.

Some people achieve their purpose by following their dream. I'm not referring here to a night dream. I am indicating following one's inner urge, the small inner voice one hears in the quiet times.

Whatever creates movement toward receiving the inner urge and acting upon the inner urge fulfills the purpose of life.

Thought to remember:
  Purpose is a natural extension of the mind to explore meaning.
  Thought is the factor for anything coming into being.

What to do:
  Observe and be aware of your thoughts.

Chapter 4
Keys for Discovering Your Purpose in Life

1. Desire to know one's purpose. Therefore, contemplation is the beginning of formulating the desire.

2. Cause the mind to be receptive, to receive what is needed.

3. Identify and create a clear image of the purpose.

4. Remember and then practice purpose in all life circumstances.

5. Identify in the present moment what is being added.

6. The continual practice of building understandings.

7. The passing on to others so that wisdom and mastery can be gained.

8. A disciplined mind and mastery of the thoughts.

9. A still mind.

10. Pure consciousness - Self beyond mind thought.

**More keys for discovering and fulfilling
your purpose in life.**

1. Look to areas that have always been of interest to you.

2. Remember your childhood dreams and aspirations.

3. Remember the main role you played in the imaginary games you played by yourself as a child.

4. Ask yourself, "What would I really like to be doing with my life if money were not a factor?"

5. Review your life. Were there any major forks in the road? Are you glad of the choices you made? Is it too late to choose differently?

6. Still your mind and receive all new information that comes your way. Examine ideas to discover if they really are of interest to you.

7. Persevere. Once you have chosen to act on an idea, persevere. Be committed.

8. Keep improving. Learn from each step of fulfilling your destiny. Keep learning. Add the new learning to what you already know, thereby increasing your ability to move toward fulfilling your purpose for being here on mother Earth.

9. Realize you are always in a state of becoming. Therefore, use each day's experience to become more than you were yesterday.

10. Create an ideal image of yourself. Create a clear, strong thought of who you want to be and what you want to become.

11. Use every experience to build your confidence, love, security, truth, value, discipline, receptivity, trust, determination and caring. Build your enlightenment.

12. Practice making clear mental images. Everything begins with a thought. Everything is created from thought. Therefore, control and direct your thoughts productively.

13. Eliminate all negative thinking from your consciousness. Negative thoughts and negative thinking only serve to hold a person back. Negative thinking slows one down and gets in the way of fulfilling one's destiny, one's purpose in life.

Stages of Growth

In order to understand and master the keys to purpose in life, one needs to know the stages of growth and their qualities. I wrote about these stages extensively in my book, <u>The Stages of Growth</u>.

There are four stages of growth. By knowing their qualities, one is able to determine what stage one is in and use that stage to the fullest.

The four stages of growth are:
1. Infancy
2. Adolescence
3. Adulthood
4. Wisdom

The qualities of the stage of growth known as infancy are:

openness	innocence
absorption	trust
curiosity	love

Openness is a quality of infancy because the brain and conscious mind are new and the inner Self, the subconscious mind is eager to learn. There is an awareness of space for learning within the Self that needs to be filled.

Absorption is a quality of infancy because there is a complete need to understand, accomplish and receive into the Self. There is a need to experience and receive the knowledge, understanding and wisdom from the experiences.

Innocence is a quality of infancy due to the fact that there is a void or lack of experience. There is an openness, a willingness to receive from all areas of experience of life and of existence.

Trust flows from innocence. Trust is a quality of infancy because trust is a natural part of expression, and trust promotes openness of Self.

Love is a quality of infancy because love is the fuel that is at the core of all forms of growth. The essence of every child is permeated with love. Love powers the need to learn and grow rapidly. Infancy is the time of most rapid growth in the brain and body.

Receptivity manifests itself in all the qualities of infancy.

Openness is the opportunity to receive all.

Absorption is the opportunity to receive and absorb the learning.

Curiosity stimulates motion in order to have the experiences needed to receive the learning.

Innocence allows the ability to receive without any fears or doubts to block receptivity.

Trust enables the Self to remain open to receive.

Love continues to permit there to be openness of the Self and to find joy in the learning.

If you find yourself in a new experience, job, club or organization, remember to use these qualities of infancy. Be open to the experience and receive the learning.

In all four stages of growth, love is essential. To achieve the full manifestation and flowering of each stage of growth the open, nurturing quality of Love must be given, shared and received.

Infancy is a time of beginning. Each day is a new beginning. Each day is an opportunity for completion. Experience the joy of learning new things, receiving new ideas and loving life.

The qualities of the stage of growth known as adolescence are:

experimentation	action
curiosity	independence
questioning	

Experimenting is a quality of the stage of growth called adolescence because at this stage some learning has already taken place. It is through experimentation that one learns the why and how of experience. One more clearly chooses and understands what is being learned.

Curiosity is a quality of adolescence as well as infancy because this is the action that stimulates motion of all forms.

Questioning is a quality of adolescence because the type and degree of questioning is in relation to the amount of information that has been accumulated. Questioning indicates a desire to fit ideas and concepts together, to understand how something functions.

Action is a quality of adolescence because this is the way one can produce experiences usable for learning. Motion towards needs, desires or goals enables one to move into the experiences needed in order to receive the learning.

Independence is a quality of adolescence. It is in this stage that the person is beginning to formulate an idea of Self. What has been learned stimulates the urge to understand more deeply the origin of Self.

Forming an identity separate from the parents presents itself in the second stage of growth called adolescence.

The time of adolescence is a time of transition from existence in the imagination with full receptivity to more of the attention on worldly affairs. The adolescent has gained partial understanding of responsibility.

It is important that one understand purpose when moving into adolescence. Purpose eliminates the need for rebellion. When the child receives unconditional love from the parent, he or she builds security and trust.

The greatest way to cause the most rapid motion from adolescence to adulthood is gratitude and love.

The qualities of the stage of growth known as adulthood are:

productivity	action
security	maturity

The adult produces more than he or she consumes. This productivity is the hallmark of adulthood.

As the one in adulthood continues to be productive, he finds he can create value and worth in any situation, circumstance or environment at any time. This brings security.

Security does not come from what you can accumulate. Rather, security comes from what you can produce. Productivity comes from one's ability to continually create and add to what already exists in the environment.

The reason productivity is a quality of the stage of growth known as adulthood is because it is through the practice of complete receiving, absorption and experimentation that there is understanding of how ideas, thoughts and actions produce a certain result.

Security is a quality of adulthood because much of one's security is based on permanent understandings of Self and creation that continue to be built within the Self. This is the greatest productivity.

Action is a quality of adulthood because it is the motion of the mind that produces the experiences necessary to build permanent understandings. In order to receive the learning, you must place yourself in a position to receive the learning. This requires correct choices, will, imagination and intelligence.

Maturity is a quality of adulthood because much of maturity is a product of the growing awareness and trust that continues to be built as it relates to productivity and understanding.

The adult produces more than he or she consumes.

The adult produces and creates. The greatest expression of adulthood is in giving to the world to uplift the consciousness of the planet. The adult is a creator.

The adult creates, builds and adds to what already exists. The adult is open to others, knowing that in order to give to others he or she must open the self up and give from the heart. For the heart is love. The heart gives and receives love. The heart is your center of permanent understandings stored in subconscious mind as permanent memory.

The qualities of the stage of growth known as wisdom are:
peace	objectivity
longevity	identity

Peace is a quality of the stage of growth known as wisdom because at this stage there is centeredness in the Self. There is an awareness of where one has come from. There is a still and disciplined mind in the present. It is through this state of awareness that peace is produced.

Longevity is a quality of wisdom because this is connected

to what has been understood, given, and continued to grow through the results of one's efforts throughout the life.

Objectivity is a quality of wisdom due to the awareness and the building of understanding of Self as a unique individual yet intimately connected to the environment and all humanity.

Identity is a quality of wisdom due to the connectedness within the origin of Self, the essence of one's being which is I AM.

In order to achieve wisdom, it is necessary to teach the knowledge you have received and gained. Wisdom is caused by the willingness to give.

As more knowledge is gained in adulthood and passed on or taught to others, the stage is set for the movement into wisdom.

As the one in wisdom continues to teach on a higher and higher level the complete flowering of and fulfillment of wisdom is achieved. This is the movement to enlightenment.

Life is full of opportunities. However, until we give freely we fail to recognize most of these.

You don't have to wait until you are physically old in order to be wise. You can gain wisdom anytime you are willing to teach, share and give of what you have learned freely and without reservation, with an open heart and full of Love.

Thought to remember

Develop purpose in order to be aware of the opportunities in life.

What to do

Use the stages of growth to discover your purpose.

Chapter 5
Giving, Listening and Receiving
Your Inner Purpose

I asked some students I teach the following question:

What is it that you don't want to hear?

These are the answers to that question.

Student: "I don't want to hear that I am unable to understand the nature of my existence and that I am unacceptable."

My response: You need to honestly recognize your value so that you can give to humanity with your ego in the proper place.

Student: "I don't want to hear my own condemning thoughts or other people's condemning thoughts. I heard Dr. Dan say that I need courage and I need to replace condemning thoughts with something positive. My Health Analysis suggested meditating on courage. My inner mind told me I need gratitude for my experiences and compassion for myself and others."

My response: Condemnation closes the heart. Acceptance and compassion open the heart.

Student: "I don't want to hear others tell me I can't do something. I'm working on hearing more of what everyone has to say."

My response: The undisciplined imagination creates fear. It is necessary and important to shine the light of attention on the thoughts or parts of yourself that you would rather not see. Then you can admit, become aware and change.

Student: "I don't want to hear that I am alone."

My response: Everyone is important. It requires honesty to admit the value one has to give to the world. The enlightened world teachers all admitted the value of what they had to give.

Purpose is personal benefit. Choose, create and cause yourself to have purpose in each activity.

Purpose or personal benefit has to change from fear and protection to something higher, greater and more enlightening.

Purpose needs to include learning. The desire to know and learn must be greater than the desire to be right or wrong.

To build permanent learning or understanding in the Self you must build a greater connectedness with life and with people.

Permanent learning or understanding is not built by avoidance.

The desire to know, the desire to build understandings, must be stronger than the fear of being destroyed.

The only true solution to life is to learn or receive the lesson and the learning in each experience. Purpose creates a state of mind in which one is open to receive a personal benefit. Therefore, creating purpose helps the mind open to receive.

A productive affirmation to promote purpose or personal benefit thinking is: **"I am always learning. Every experience adds to me and gives me more, always more and greater truth, love, LIGHT and awareness."**

The evolving consciousness imagines and creates greater and greater purposes. In other words, as you grow in awareness, understanding and enlightenment then your purposes evolve.

A job or money alone may no longer satisfy you. You want more say so or decision making ability in your job and your life. You want more fulfillment. You want to know the meaning of life. These are higher purposes. These are purposes beyond physical, tangible, sensory things. These are purposes or qualities that affect the inner being.

Each and every experience, no matter how seemingly small or insignificant can have a purpose.

Creating a purpose for doing the little, seemingly insignificant or unimportant things for the Self and others prepares the way for the greater and powerful singular ideal and purpose of knowing the whole Self. To know the whole Self is to be enlightened and have the true and lasting fulfillment.

Creating purpose consistently every day prepares the way for the singular purpose of <u>knowing</u> the one <u>true</u> reality and transcending entrapment in a physical body and physical life.

An ideal is an image of what you want to become or be.

A goal is a visualized benefit.

Activity is work, energy expended, effort or physical motion.

When creating ideals and meaningful purposes, it is important to be specific. If the imaged purpose is nebulous you will either get a nebulous creation that is not specific enough to serve you or your creation will be so nebulous that you will hardly recognize it.

It is vital that you see, or perceive, how what you are dong (activity) is going to benefit you and move you closer to what you want to become.

What you are <u>doing</u>, which is activity, should add to your awareness, understanding and wisdom and move you forward to what you want to <u>become</u>.

Therefore, each day be consistent in achieving, accomplishing and going beyond limitations. Accomplish a goal. Fulfill a purpose. Discipline your mind and be committed to adding to yourself.

There are two kinds of motivation.

1. **Inner motivation**
2. **Outer motivation**

Outer motivation comes from the physical environment. The physical environment provides sensory stimulus. This stimulus then leads to physical desires. When the desires are met a person temporarily feels good or has a gratifying sensory experience. The rest of the time one has a craving or an unhappiness or a feeling of lack of fulfillment.

Inner motivation comes from purpose. This is because purpose, which is personal benefit, provides desire and desire provides motivation.

The wonderful thing about purpose is you are never dependent upon the environment to provide motivation. You can create your own motivation anytime and at all times.

To be dependent on the outer environment for motivation means that sometimes you will have it and sometimes you will not have it. It is not reasonable to put the control and power outside of yourself. Therefore, create purpose every day. Imagine useful beneficial purposes every day for the things you do.

It is important to have a purpose that is of benefit in the moment, in the now. The present is the only place that one can learn, grow and be fulfilled. The present, the now, the eternal now, is the only time and place that one can gain permanent understandings of Self and creation. The present is the only time one can gain lasting growth and enlightenment.

It is important to be specific in the visualization and imaging of ideal and purpose. This is how real learning can be caused to occur more rapidly. The stronger and more specific the image the more the subconscious mind has to work with.

In being specific one becomes more committed to achieving one's ideal and purpose. It is too easy to generalize and deny you've achieved a goal. Also by generalizing you may try to take credit for something you really didn't create. So being specific keeps you honest.

Being specific in imaging, visualizing, and describing your thoughts and purposes helps to build one's self value and self esteem because you have proven to yourself what you have created.

As long as the thought is nebulous it is too easy to allow the mind to be passive and to lose sight of the ideal and purpose. Therefore it becomes harder to gain the learning from an experience.

Being specific with one's ideal and purpose enables one to appreciate structure. This enables one to build greater alignment and flexibility in the physical body.

Ideals, goals and purposes must relate to the present in some way. This is because the present, the now, is the only place one can change, learn and grow in awareness.

Purpose is to be renewed, strengthened, improved and built upon each day.

Each day stretch and reach not only to achieve more but to be more than you were yesterday. To grow in consciousness and awareness is to reach and stretch beyond the accepted limitations of yesterday.

In order for purpose to provide motivation it must be something that is important to you.

Purpose defines the value of your experiences. Creating purpose is a choice. No one else creates purpose for you. Others may provide education, or stimulation, or instruction. Yet, ultimately the individual chooses the purpose.

Creating purpose is an exercise of one's imagination and

determines how quickly one will evolve. Have or create a clear image of who you want to become through your effort and activity and the benefit you will receive from that activity.

The Simple, Little Things Lead to the Big Things

Each day each person can make hundreds of decisions or else go on habitual auto pilot and make very few new, original decisions.

To make a decision requires one to choose a thought.

It is the little thoughts and little decisions that lead to successful, great thoughts that lead to great decisions.

Don't wait for the event to arrive and then wonder why you can't handle it. Rather make conscious decisions each day that cause you to stretch and go beyond previously accepted limitations. In the process you will expand beyond previously accepted limitations and thereby become capable of handling the greater decisions and responsibilities.

Soul growth or reaching one's full potential in many ways concerns expanding one's options, while refusal to change is avoiding options.

Remember, experiences are essentially neutral.

One's thoughts, attitudes and consciousness in relation to the experience determines not only the physical outcome but also the learning and growth in awareness gained from the experience.

It is your thoughts and attitudes that determine what you get out of an experience.

Mental discipline is the key to overriding one's limitations in consciousness.

Mental discipline produces, over time, a still mind.

A still mind is the key to knowing and fulfilling one's life purpose.

True purpose is always grounded in truth, because purpose aligns with Universal Truth.

Purpose motivates because in gaining personal benefits one has the opportunity to gain greater truth.

Consistent, constant mental discipline leads to eternal, personal and lasting truth, awareness, understanding, and love.

The purpose of Love is to promote a greater connectedness between individuals.

In order to grow and progress rapidly in the fulfillment of life's purpose, one must grow in love and compassion.

Where does purpose come from? Purpose comes from the imagination of the thinker. Purpose is created by imaging or visualizing purposes in all that you do.

People that are physically minded and rely mostly on memory often feel like life has no meaning or purpose. This is because the purpose of life is not fulfilled in the brain.

The purpose of life is fulfilled by aligning the conscious and subconscious minds and attuning them to superconscious mind. Then the Self can fully experience the present moment as I AM.

To fulfill purpose one must first imagine purpose. Productive imagination requires using and directing the mind.

Purpose helps the individual improve the ability to assimilate the learning in each experience to a higher degree.

Purpose, which is personal benefit, keeps the attention on being able to assimilate the truth into oneself.

As one continues to regularly initiate purposes, the benefits evolve from food, shelter and clothing to great insights into

Universal Truth, as well as wisdom, awareness, understanding, love and enlightenment.

As the individual evolves into achieving the great purpose of life and full potential the inner urge to give to others and aid others increases. Over time such a one's giving increases to become a world teacher and a world server. Then the purpose becomes universal.

The greatest personal benefit is a purpose that adds to the whole, permanent Self.

It is universally true that, as you give so shall you receive. By creating purpose a person is in position to give more and receive more.

As you give to others you receive the great abundance and treasures of high knowledge from the universe.

Because the true nature of reality is connectedness one who gives more aligns with the true reality to a greater degree.

Question — How can I discover my purpose in life?
Answer — Still your mind and listen.

Some people are more motivated by thinking about ideals and activities that will benefit other people. How can this kind of person be motivated for personal benefit?

The answer is self value, self worth, self esteem and self respect. By being willing to look at situations and circumstances from a different perspective one can perceive personal benefits, purpose, in a new way. This can be motivating.

Also by admitting one's value in giving, one finds it is easier to receive higher truths into the Self. Receiving higher truth and understanding is also motivating.

Look for the learning in each experience. Receive the learning in each experience. Learn to find joy in each experience and enjoy the learning.

Also enjoy sharing your learning with others. Then there will be a stronger desire to learn more because you have more to share with others.

To fulfill one's purpose in life requires discipline, concentration and imagination as well as improving one's memory. It is not necessary that you develop a photographic memory. It is necessary and important that you develop an honest and useful memory.

What is an honest and useful memory? An honest and useful memory is one that can be used to make you a better person, a more loving person, a more truth-filled person, a more enlightened person.

A dishonest memory will blame others for past failures. A dishonest memory will hold grudges.

An honest memory will remember those events, thoughts, situations and words of the past that were productive. The one with an honest memory will seek to emulate these memory thoughts, actions and words. Such a one will seek to build upon what is productive and fulfilling.

It is very important to learn to discipline oneself. There is great value in creatively designing ways to discipline the Self.

One of my Self imposed disciplines was the practice of never saying a not or no. In other words I practiced the discipline of eliminating all negative words from my vocabulary. I practiced this discipline of choosing positive over negative words for three years. After three years I found that I now had control of negative words. In other words, I could use them when necessary and use them correctly without misusing the words no and not.

Mental discipline gives one the ability to make the right choices at the right times.

People tend to practice avoidance. Sometimes they avoid the things they most need to learn. Everyone needs to learn the Universal Lessons of life. So why do most people avoid them?

They avoid the experiences that require extra effort. People tend to avoid the experiences that make them uncomfortable.

An open mind is required to accept something new in one's life and consciousness, especially new ideas. New ideas represent a threat to what has come before to a person with a closed mind. This is why people with new ideas are sometimes attacked or vilified by those entrenched in the status quo.

Thus it is that if you are to be attached to any one thing let that attachment be to growthful change and the expansion of awareness, which is attachment to enlightenment.

Experiences must be received into the Self in order for learning to occur. Lessons of life, lessons of Self, lessons of Universal Laws and Truths can be integrated into one's consciousness each day.

People tend to have an experience or go through an experience without learning the lesson that an experience affords. I have spent over a quarter of a century teaching people how to learn the lessons of mental evolution and enlightenment through their experiences. I have also taught people how to cause experiential learning that affords the Self an opportunity for greater learning.

A key to gleaning the learning in your life is to ask yourself, "What am I learning in this situation? What am I learning in this experience?"

Gratitude

Gratitude and thankfulness are very powerful tools for increasing one's ability to learn.

Gratitude increases one's ability to receive.

Gratitude increases one's ability to receive the abundance of the universe.

To be thankful indicates one has already received something of value. Receptivity, the ability to receive, is a powerful key to deriving the essential learning in every experience.

Thought to remember:
Being closed off or blaming others causes one to miss out on the learning in life. Therefore, use gratitude as a tool to open the Self to greater love and greater learning.

What to do:
Improve your listening abilities.

Chapter 6
Outer and Inner Purpose

When you have only outer purpose then you will want to find new things to do all the time. You will like and want to do new things. If you have to do them over and over for many months you will get bored and want to do something else. You will have fulfilled your temporary desire that was based on an outward stimulus. Physical experience and physical pleasure are always temporary.

Whereas, creating purpose for all you do, or anything you do, can give you an inexhaustible well of desire and need fulfillment. And your desires will change as you evolve and grow.

<u>Outer Physical Purposes and Inner Mental Purposes</u>

In the journey of life we learn to use our physical body and five senses. We learn what is pleasurable and what is painful. We learn to have motivation to achieve what is pleasurable. This motivation is seen as personal benefit or purpose.

For example, you may have an urge toward a higher paying job. What are the benefits of a higher paying job? The higher paying job will give you the money to buy a newer car or a larger house or more expensive clothes. These are all physical personal benefits or purposes.

There is nothing wrong with physical purpose as long as you don't stay there. In other words, it is each person's inherent right and duty to progress to a greater, a more evolved state of consciousness.

Therefore, purpose or personal benefit must evolve also. After you have taken care of your basic physical needs it is time to progress to taking care of your mental, spiritual or consciousness needs.

The outer or physical purpose gives you the motivation to achieve your physical goals in the future.

The inner or mental purpose gives you the motivation to achieve your ideals in the eternal now.

Physical goals and physical purposes can take up so much of your attention that you may miss the inner purpose.

The inner purpose isn't about what you are doing. It's about how you are doing the activity. It is about your thought, your discipline, your stillness of the mind. Are your thoughts repetitive and habitual or are they involved in imaging and visualizing your future?

The quality of your consciousness in the present moment determines everything.

The outer or physical purpose belongs to the horizontal dimension of space and time. It is of the physical world.

The inner or vertical purpose is of the now and involves a deepening of one's ability to benefit the whole Self, the whole consciousness, and the whole being.

The inner purpose is a moment by moment choice to add to one's consciousness.

These continual choices to add to one's self and one's consciousness create the movement, the transformation to enlightenment.

Inner purpose gives one lasting fulfillment. Outer purpose gives one temporary stimulation or satisfaction.

As one grows in awareness through the fulfillment of inner purpose the inner LIGHT of one's consciousness fills one's being and becomes more and more apparent.

Purpose is never negative. Thus purpose is not stated with a not.

It would be incorrect to state one's purpose as:

> My purpose is not to get married.
> *or* My purpose is to not to be part of the group.
> *or* My purpose is to not listen.

A purpose is a personal benefit. Therefore, purpose is about what you will learn or add to your Self, your being, your consciousness.

> A purpose can be to gain or learn Self value.
> A purpose can be to learn receptivity.
> A purpose can be to build will power.
> A purpose can be to build compassion.

When is life worth living?

Life is worth living in the now.

Now is where and when you can have purpose.
Now is where you can benefit.

When is life worth living?
> In the now.

When you give moment to moment.
When you experience love.
When you give love.
When you receive love.
When you have purpose.
When you learn something that is permanent and lasting.
When you are aware of growth.

What we are here to do in life is to know truth and love. To know truth and love is to give and receive truth and love.

To learn is to receive truth into the Self for greater connectedness and greater consciousness.

Love makes truth easy to receive.

The more one comes to know the Self the greater one's purpose and awareness of purpose.

This is because one's purpose goes beyond the physical life. Purpose also includes the mental and emotional life.

Practice expanding attention beyond the Self. As this is practiced, one comes to know the Self as more than a physical body.

Discipline is the way to direct the mind to know the Self. Discipline is required in order to expand one's consciousness.

Each moment is an opportunity to practice enlightenment. Each moment is an opportunity to practice purpose.

How does one gain the motivation to discipline the whole mind? The answer is purpose.

Your essence is LIGHT. Each learning, each adding to one's consciousness is a growth into the LIGHT of understanding and awareness.

In order to know the true nature of LIGHT one must master the still mind.

Your greatest friend is a still and disciplined mind.

This is because from a disciplined mind one can choose to be either aggressive or receptive. From a disciplined mind one can learn at a more rapid rate. From the still mind one can receive the higher consciousness.

Success is gaining greater enlightenment every day.

In order for any individual to become fulfilled, ideal and purpose must align. This means that your personal benefit, purpose, must become one with what you want to be or become.

I have discovered that the greatest personal benefit is En-LIGHT-enment. What I want to be and become is enlightened. Therefore, my ideal and purpose are singular.

The full flowering of the physical Self into the Divine or Enlightened Self must occur. Therefore, make it your ideal to be or become enlightened. It is a state of being, a state of consciousness.

We are LIGHT in essence and at the core of our being. Even the physical body is made up of atoms which are made up of a nucleus with electrons circling at a vast distance.

Therefore, most of our outer universe and most of our inner universe is empty space. The power to fulfill your purpose in life is to use LIGHT and space. Your light, the individual's light, is the LIGHT of awareness.

Therefore, in order to fulfill your purpose make each day an opportunity for learning and the growth of awareness. Let light fill your being and expand into the space within your body and within your mind.

You may begin by visualizing or imaging your body filled with LIGHT. See and perceive the electronic interplay of energy forces within your body. All within the space.

There is a great potentiality in space. It is important to fill it with your LIGHT.

As we create with others, share with others, give and receive with others, we share not only our inner light but also we share our space.

This sharing of lights and space we call love.

When two people have like ideals and like purposes they often become life partners. Their love for life grows and they grow together. As they grow together their capacity to give and receive love to each other grows.

The ideal is who and what you want to become. It is the evolutionary impulse. As two people, who are marriage partners, move forward in achieving their ideal Self, their love for each other grows and matures. Each finds a greater light, a greater love and a boundless space in each other.

The will is your ability to choose your experiences and to choose to be in those experiences with awareness.

The imagination is your ability to direct your consciousness to greater learning and new or greater creation.

Together the will and imagination can accomplish greater wonders and can fulfill your life's purpose.

Purpose is personal benefit.

There are benefits of all kinds. There are physical benefits. There are emotional benefits.

What is the value of life without purpose?

Most people do not know the purpose of life because they live in the world of the senses. The five physical senses can only give you a physical purpose to life because they only sense, receive and perceive physical things.

However, the real purpose of life is not physical because physical life is temporary.

The real purpose of life brings lasting and permanent fulfillment. How then is it possible to know this purpose that is beyond physical, sensory experience?

The answer lies in the proper and productive use of the mind, the attention, the will, and the imagination.

The mind is the vehicle, your vehicle for knowing the Self.

The will is the ability to make continuous choices toward a goal or ideal.

The imagination is the ability to image or visualize what one wants to create.

The attention is your ability to fully learn in each experience and use the mind.

You are a valuable and important person. Purpose causes one to realize this because purpose is personal benefit.

Having purpose is the ability to image a benefit in the willful activity. To gain the benefit one must be willing to receive the benefit.

Thought to remember:

Open your mind and heart to receive the love, LIGHT and truth into yourself.

What to do:

Practicing creating purpose in all you do. Ask yourself, "What is my purpose for each activity, each experience?"

Chapter 7

Sharing, Opening Up and Purpose
Sharing and Success

To experience life more abundantly one must be open hearted and open minded. In this way one is willing to approach life differently every day. Such a one is willing to open the Self up to other people every day. Such a one is willing to share and to both give and receive with others. In some cases one is willing to receive on a level and with a depth that one was not willing to before.

Most people would like to have greater successes. Few realize that greater success often means opening the Self up to the bounty and abundance of the Universe. Success may also mean opening oneself up to greater love. Greater love improves the quality of one's life. Most everyone wants to improve their station or condition in life.

Sometimes success is a matter of thinking differently. Thinking differently may at times be more important than doing things differently.

Thought is Cause

It is through our thoughts that we change our life. It is through our thoughts that we create our life. It is through our thoughts that we have created our life up to the present time.

Some people want to change the world. If you want to change the world then you must first change yourself. If you would change your Self you must change your thoughts. To change your thoughts is to elevate your thoughts to a higher perspective. This higher perspective is one of Love, LIGHT, Truth and connectedness.

The people and situations in life tend to change over time. People die or move away. You attract to you people of like mind, or similar learning.

A good gauge of whether you are changing is the degree to which the kind of people around you changes. As your thoughts improve people of a more productive or enlightened nature will be drawn into your sphere of influence.

You attract people and other people are attracted to you. People are attracted to what you have to say and offer, and you become attracted or drawn to a different kind of person because of different and more elevated thoughts.

Did you know that you chose your parents before you were born? To someone thinking physically this idea seems preposterous. The thinking goes something like this, "How could I have chosen my parent before birth? I didn't even exist then!" To which I reply, "Of course you existed before birth! Do you think you are only an animal that lives for a few short years on Earth and then faces annihilation and oblivion?" That doesn't make any sense. You have the ability to choose now and you had the ability to choose before you were born and you will have the ability to choose after you withdraw your attention from physical life, which is commonly called death.

If everyone in this country would accept that we choose our parents before birth it would totally revolutionize the consciousness of this planet.

It means so much for people to not only realize and accept they chose their parents but also to realize and know why they chose their parents.

The parents you chose for this lifetime are your first teachers. Even if you do not appreciate some of the things they said or did. Remember, your parents not only gave you your early education, they also gave you the stimulus to look for greater understanding. That is why you are reading this book.

The truth that you chose your parents is an idea whose time has come. It is a mental image of the truth that you are an eternal being and you existed before you inhabited this physical body and you will exist after you cease to inhabit and use this physical body. Therefore, you have the ability to choose whether you are in a physical body or not.

Whether a person achieves greatness or mediocrity is a matter of that person's thoughts.

Whether a person fulfills the purpose of life or their purpose in life, is a matter of that person's thoughts.

The choices you make are a result of the thoughts you think.

The life you live is a result of the choices you make which are a result of the thoughts you think.

Listen to the words you say for they reveal your thoughts. As you become more aware of your thoughts you can evaluate their value and productivity. Constantly uproot the unproductive weed thoughts and replace them with truth filled and loving fruitful thoughts.

A productive goal can be of help to the individual because it directs the mind in a productive manner.

A goal is something physical that you want to achieve.

You may have a goal to sweep the floor or run a mile or pay your bills. These are all actions that you want to achieve.

An ideal is what you want to become.

A goal is what you want to do and in doing you achieve.

An ideal is what you want to be, and in being you become.

If you want to become enlightened then let that be your ideal.

If you say, "I want to be loving," then let that be your ideal of what you want to be.

Goals don't provide motivation. Because of this, when someone gives you a goal often there is no motivation.

Therefore, a purpose is needed with the goal. Purpose provides motivation because purpose is personal benefit. Purpose provides desire and motivation that wells up from deep within.

The desires that are stimulated from physical objects are usually temporary and only provide temporary satisfaction.

The desires that come from within and from purpose are more long lasting and can be constantly regenerated.

Desires are endless because each new physical situation or object can provide a new stimulus which creates a new desire.

However, desires only provide temporary satisfaction or happiness and then you are left wanting more.

As one creates more purpose in the life the desires begin coming from within. Then these inner desires evolve the need to know Self, Mind and consciousness. In other words, the desires evolve from temporary to the permanent and lasting.

By choosing thoughts that align with Universal Laws and Universal Truths one's life takes on a more permanent and lasting quality. This is a powerful <u>key</u> to developing the deepening, enlightened, <u>purpose filled life</u>.

Honesty leads to truth which leads to Universal Truth.

Truth overcomes fear because fear is of the darkness and truth brings LIGHT to the world.

Love and truth overcome hatred, anger, and all negativity.

The more you practice purpose, the more your purpose elevates. The more your purpose elevates, the more you understand your purpose in life.

As long as you have mostly physical purposes you will probably have mostly physical goals and you probably won't have many ideals. So the solution is to always strive to elevate your thoughts. Elevate your giving and receiving. This requires discipline.

How to Use the Mind and the Brain

It requires discipline to choose a thought other than the ones you are habituated to.

To <u>choose</u> a different thought is to use your mind.

To think the same thoughts, day after day is to be engrossed and entrapped in your physical brain.

Which do you choose to use, the brain or the mind?

If you choose the brain you will rely mostly on memory.

If you rely mostly on the mind you will know and value the present moment. You will also create a different and greater future.

If you choose to use both the mind and the brain you will reason well because you will effectively use memory, attention, and imagination. You will use the senses correctly. You will use attention correctly. You will receive the most truth-filled learning from every situation and experience.

To become more awake to life is to increase one's choices while decreasing one's unconscious functioning from habit.

The degree to which one functions from habit is the degree to which one is asleep. Habits are faint memories from the past. The past is not the same as the present.

To treat the past the same as the present is to lack or be ineffective at reasoning because the past is not the same as the present.

Each moment is unique to itself.

Therefore, the only truly effective and reasoning way to function is to be in the present moment. **It is in the present moment that one finds, creates and fulfills purpose.**

It is in the present moment that one has a productive use of memory.

It is in the present moment that one imagines and therefore creates a greater future.

One who functions from habit is, to that degree, unconscious and therefore misinterprets the now, the present.

To choose to discipline the mind and to cause greater awareness may at times seem difficult. Why make a choice to grow in awareness or enlightenment when it seems difficult? Because what you receive will be more than worth the effort.

Comfortableness never caused growth in awareness or expansion of consciousness. Comfortableness never caused enlightenment. Comfortableness never caused one to understand the purpose of life.

To discipline one's Self and one's mind creates the possibility of creating one's fondest desires, needs and dreams.

To discipline one's mind gives one a much greater opportunity to fulfill one's purpose.

To discipline one's mind gives the capability to use each moment, the present moment, to the fullest.

When the environment stimulates the desire it is sometimes called stimulus and response. An animal often acts according to stimulus and response.

When creating a purpose you make a choice that comes from deep within. This way a desire from within is achieved.

There is fulfillment that can be achieved through new experience. To make the same choice based upon memory is to create the same or similar experiences over and over.

Use the imagination, the imaginative faculty, to create a greater purpose.

The brain and conscious ego rebel against discipline because they receive less sensory stimulation. The brain and conscious ego work with or function with the physical body. The physical body or animal body wants and seeks pleasure and attempts to avoid pain. It is important to make something other than sensory stimulation your highest priority in life.

Concentration and meditation do not necessarily offer physical sensory pleasure. While practicing concentration the individual attention is not on sensory pleasure. Instead the attention is directed to a single point of focus in concentration or a single point of stillness in meditation.

To be awake is to not only know one's thoughts but also to choose one's thoughts or to choose no thought by stilling the mind.

To function from habits, which are brain pathways, is to be unconscious of one's thoughts and motives.

To function from environmental stimulus is to be compulsive. Stimulus and response puts the power outside the Self in the environment.

To create a desire from a Self created purpose is to be conscious and to have the power of choice. This power of choice comes from within you.

Why make a choice that is difficult or seems difficult? It seems easier to be comfortable and to stay the same.

There is fulfillment that can be experienced through thinking a new thought and making a different decision.

Use the imagination, the imaginative faculty, to create a greater purpose for an uncomfortable choice.

Evaluate your thoughts. What is your main limitation in consciousness?

Fear, doubt, anger, jealousy, greed, and resentment are limitations in consciousness. Becoming Self absorbed and dwelling in negative thinking only slows one's progress in understanding and fulfilling life's purpose. If left alone, the passivity of self can lead to isolation, depression and prolonged suffering.

Most Self absorption comes from dwelling in the past. You don't always need to figure out the past in order to fulfill your purpose in the present, although at times it may help.

By choosing to place one's attention on the present experience one can learn, change, grow and thereby release the limitations of the past.

The only place to learn and to expand one's consciousness is in the present. The only time to fulfill one's purpose is in the now.

In placing the attention fully in the present the limitations of one's past are released.

The mind loves to create problems and then try to find solutions to those problems. So therefore, when the mind is still, the mind stops creating problems to be solved. The mind will not do this on its own because the mind wants to get to do things. It wants to create problems and solve them.

To allow the mind to become busy is to create a main limitation in consciousness. The lack of having a still mind is the cause of all great limitations in life. The scattered mind may seem to function as a defense or barrier between oneself and others, yet it only isolates you. A scattered mind enables one to avoid looking at what one finds unpleasant or fearful. A scattered mind is a fearful mind.

The scattered mind causes you to forget who you really are and to miss the purpose of life.

Opening Up

In order to discover and know your purpose in life you will have to open up. Most people find this idea frightening. This is because most people live in or carry some kind of fear around with them. Yet a flower doesn't fear opening up. A flower bud finds fulfillment in opening up to the sun.

A newborn baby is fully open to learning. Children are open to learning. Yet as people age most people begin to close themselves off. By this I mean that they accept fear into their consciousness or way of thinking.

Fear causes one to want to protect the Self. This protective thinking creates a barrier around the Self that inhibits and restricts one's ability to receive new learning into the Self.

The fear-based person becomes like the flower bud that refuses to open up to the light of day.

All plants need sunlight. If we use the term light as a metaphor for awareness then it becomes obvious that each person needs more light of awareness in order to progress and grow as a spiritual being.

How can one receive greater awareness and understanding? The answer is to decide to choose to be completely open to receive the learning in whatever life presents to us. Our life is a series of choices not only to give but also to receive.

Sharing
Creating a Purpose for One's Life

Purpose provides or creates motivation because purpose is personal benefit. So what does one do to motivate the Self to create a purpose for the life?

To create a purpose for your life, place your attention on giving or sharing what you have and what you know.

You can begin your sharing by giving in small ways and then build up to giving in larger ways.

Everyone has a skill, talent, ability, wisdom or learning that can be shared with others. Begin with the area you are most confident with sharing. ASK questions and listen. Find out what people are interested in. Let people know the abilities and awareness you possess.

A higher purpose is always created in conjunction with other people.

Will Power and Determination

Will power is indispensable to achieve your purpose in life. Will power is the continuous choice to go towards the imaged desire that you have been creating. Will power success in life is dependent upon being able to sustain initiative.

People have difficulty completing things.

Most failures are at the end. It may seem difficult to bring your ideas into full manifestation and completion because that would mean or indicate that you would need to admit a greater capacity for creating. You would need to go beyond limitations.

Reasons for Failure

People fail in a number of ways.

1. They fail to have a clear image that they can be committed to achieving.

It is difficult to achieve a goal if you do not have a clear image in the mind's eye of what you want to achieve.

2. People fail to recognize enough value in themselves. They, therefore, do not believe they are worthy of achieving and accomplishing.

3. People fail to complete what they begin. They fail at the end. Sometimes they just give up too early.

What is the connection of desires to purpose since this book's subject is purpose?

There are two kinds of desires:

1. Desires generated from outer, environmental stimulus.

2. Desires created from Self-created inner purpose.

Outer desires are fleeting and temporary.

Desires generated from purpose can give permanent understanding and lasting benefit to the individual creating them.

Purpose provides desires and motivation by providing a personal benefit. When you create purpose you have a personal benefit in mind.

Desires without the personal motivation to achieve them are helpless wishes floating away in the wind.

1. There are physical desires.

2. And there are mental desires.

Physical desires give temporary satisfaction. Emotional desires give relief and joy. Mental desires give fulfillment.

Mental desires are concerned with fulfilling the real Self, the inner Self, the permanent Self. Mental desires encompass one's learning of the whole Self.

As one evolves, one's physical desires evolve more and

more into mental needs. Every person has a real need for greater awareness and enlightenment.

Without purpose life has little or no meaning. Without purpose in each experience, that experience has little or no meaning, and even less fulfillment.

Without purpose goals are empty. You may achieve a goal but without purpose what lasting satisfaction is there? Without purpose where is the motivation to achieve a goal? In most cases it is lacking.

Therefore, it is important to create a purpose for those goals and ideals we desire to achieve in life.

Write your purpose on paper and read it out loud.

True mental, mind or whole Self learning is accomplished through the activity of physical experiences, and physical experiences are perceived and received into the brain through the five senses. Always seek to learn the life lesson, the essence in each experience. Draw that permanent learning, the essence of each experience, into the Self.

Physical experiences exist in order that we may draw the permanent learning from them. Most people only get the temporary sensory gratification.

Will power is needed and required to achieve great things in life. A great thing may be whatever you create that goes beyond your previously accepted limitations.

Will power is the continuous choice to go towards the imaged desire that you have been creating.

If you think or feel you do not have enough will power then you may be lacking in imagination. For if you can imagine something greater or better for yourself then you may begin to believe you can achieve it. By identifying one's purpose the clarity of seeing the personal benefit of something greater in one's life becomes apparent.

By imagining a purpose, the desire and greater motivation will be yours.

Self dislike or Self degradation can keep one from achieving a goal or receiving a desire.

It is important to understand the difference between believing and knowing.

Believing is the act of accepting an idea into yourself.

Knowing is the action of using that belief to create and become through experience a better person.

A good way to practice identifying the difference between believing and knowing is to ask yourself, "How do I know this or how do I know that?"

Merely separating and identifying what you believe from what you know can aid in clarifying what one needs to learn.

It is productive in learning to know your purpose in life to gain greater awareness of believing, knowing and the difference between the two.

The more you understand the power of belief the more you can understand the power of the quality of knowing.

Most people want to know their purpose in life instead of just believing they have a purpose.

When you hear yourself saying, "I know this or I know that," say, "What is it I believe about this?" Then describe out loud all the things you believe about what you just said that you know.

After you have described everything you believe about an object or subject then describe in detail what you know about that object or subject.

From this practice you will learn to identify clearly the

difference between believing and knowing which will enable you to use both of them more effectively.

The more one learns about the qualities of believing and knowing the more one will be able to use them to come to know the purpose of life.

By separating and identifying what one believes from what one knows there can be a greater commitment to what one wants to know in life. And purpose is perhaps the greatest or one of the greatest things one can know in life.

Commitment is very powerful. Until one has committed to a goal, ideal, desire or purpose in life there will always be the scattering of one's energies and attention.

Once one is committed to a principal or ideal all or most of one's energies, be they mental, emotional, or physical,0 can be directed toward achieving the goal desired.

Once one has commitment, all kinds of wonderful, seemingly chance or coincidental happenings occur to further one's movement towards receiving one's most heartfelt desires.

Successful people always have commitment in one form or another. How can one have success if there is no decision as to what will bring success. To believe or know what will bring success one must have an image, ideal, idea, or goal to be committed to achieving.

Negative or limiting thoughts indicate that one's mind does not have intelligent direction. It is not intelligent to create mental pictures or images that tear the Self down or degrade the Self.

Instead replace negative thoughts with positive productive mental images. Remember this, "the hallmark of adulthood in reasoning is that you produce more than you consume."

It is important to replace all limiting thoughts with higher truth. As you replace negative or limiting thoughts with thoughts that are in alignment with the Universal Truths and Universal Laws, your consciousness will move to greater heights of Self knowing and Self awareness.

Don't avoid. Do not avoid looking at yourself, your life, your thoughts, and your experiences. Then decide what is productive and what is unproductive. Always be ready and willing to receive a higher truth.

We are here on this Earth for the purpose of coming to know ourselves. To know the Real Self one must master one's mind. To master one's mind, one must master one's thoughts. To master one's thoughts, one must choose all thoughts and achieve a still mind. To achieve a still mind, one must practice mental disciplines such as concentration, meditation, imaging and breathwork.

Do not avoid finding out about yourself. That is the only way you will come to know who you really are. Any perceived ugliness and negativity is only temporary. Therefore, identify it and choose something more productive.

Once you can acknowledge the limited thinking you have the ability to identify and choose something more productive.

By facing and acknowledging what is temporary in yourself you can have the awareness to begin building the permanent wisdom and understanding within.

Thought to remember:
Learn the universal from the specific.
Stop making up your own little rules of life and realize there are Universal Laws of life already in place. The quicker you align your consciousness with the Universal framework and structure of creation the quicker will you find, discover, and know your purpose for this lifetime.

What to do:

     Be specific in creating purposes each day. Receive at least one new idea into yourself each day.

Chapter 8
Gratitude, Forgiveness and Purpose

The only time you can have purpose is in the present moment. The only place you can experience purpose is in the present, which is right here and now.

No one can give you purpose, but you can create it. Purpose doesn't appear automatically. A lot of people think so, yet if placed in a job or activity they find distasteful, they will have difficulty creating a purpose for that work.

Purpose gives value to the present moment and the current experience. Too often people live in either the past or the future. As people age they tend to live more and more in the past. Sometimes they daydream about a future that never was, and probably will never be.

As people go through life they tend to accumulate hurts. Sometimes a person may be hurt by another intentionally. At other times one may misinterpret an experience as hurtful when that was not what was intended by the other person at all.

To hold onto these hurts of the past keeps one's attention, or part of one's attention, locked into the past. The difficulty with this is that the only place you can live is in the present. Therefore, the more one's attention stays in the past the less capable one is of living in the present. The result is you begin to die.

Therefore, the only reasonable solution is to live in the present and only use memory when it is useful in the day-to-day functioning of your life in the present moment.

Most memory is misused in that it is not used to aid the individual in the present moment.

Gratitude and forgiveness are powerful tools to help anyone let go of the limiting past and live more effectively in the present moment.

Forgiveness works effectively by putting the forgiving individual in a position to release past grudges, angers, resentments, hatreds, and hurts of all kinds.

Some people say, "I'll forgive but I won't forget." When this happens the person making such a statement is probably not releasing attachment to past hurt. Such a person has probably decided not to take physical revenge yet is mentally still holding on to grudges.

True forgiveness never completely or fully occurs until the individual releases attachment to a past hurt.

Forgive is made up of two words. Those two words are *for* and *give*. Forgiveness never occurs until you are willing to give of yourself in ways you have never given before.

Think about this. In order for you to forgive someone who you perceived has hurt you, you must give to that person. You must give them your forgiveness. In so doing you are actually also forgiving your self and in the process, releasing the past.

By releasing the past you can live more fully in the present. You are then more alive. Perhaps you have experienced the peace and freedom that occurs once you have released the past.

The one who forgives pardons the offender. By so doing the forgiver frees the Self from his prison of Self created limitations.

Often when you are hurt mentally, emotionally or physically there is the thought or feeling that it is your fault for what happened, even if you are the one who was hurt.

Children often blame themselves for their parents' divorce. Battered wives sometimes blame themselves for their husband's abuse. Blaming oneself never caused forgiveness.

It is important and valuable to replace blaming with causing. What does this mean? It means looking to your thoughts and attitudes for the condition of your life.

Do you have a brother or a sister? Why is their life different than yours? Because they made different choices than you did. Look at all the decisions you have made in life. Those choices, those decisions, have brought you to where you are now, mentally, emotionally and physically.

Your choices are based upon your thoughts. Repeated thoughts form attitudes. Attitudes that are repeated for a long time sometimes seem to overpower one's ability to make a totally different choice in the present moment.

Therefore it is important to choose to be open to receive new thoughts and new ideas every day in order to be able to think new thoughts every day.

As you think new thoughts you are able and capable of making new decisions, new choices every day.

By learning to think new thoughts and by making new decisions you will gain greater awareness and greater understanding. You will live more fully in the present, for the present is the only place that you can truly be effective.

Forgiveness also helps you be present in the now. Gratitude then adds power and strength to forgiveness.

It is one thing to say to yourself, "I forgive so and so (insert name here) ." It is quite another thing to give gratitude for that person. It is especially difficult at first to give gratitude out loud to a person you have been holding a grudge against.

This is not to say you approve or disapprove of what that other person did or did not do. What it does say is that you are ready to release the past by valuing what you gained from the past.

It may be easy to give gratitude and thanks out loud to someone who made you feel good or who did you a favor or who consciously helped you. But to give gratitude to the person and situation that you interpreted as unpleasant requires determination, will, love, need and the desire to move to a higher state of truth and awareness.

If you have been holding resentment, anger, hatred, animosity or wrath against someone, it may be difficult at first to change this to gratitude. However, by applying fortitude with gratitude you will prevail.

When you begin stating gratitude out loud you must then say what it is you are grateful for, no matter how large or small.

As you state your gratitude out loud each day the anger, resentment, hatred and fear will subside and release. This negative thinking will have been replaced with compassion, love and the higher truth. You will be able to breathe freely again. You may notice your health improving for these negative attitudes such as hate and jealousy only hurt the one holding these thoughts.

Negative, destructive thoughts always return to the one holding negative thoughts. Positive, productive, caring thoughts always return to the one holding and producing those thoughts. That is a powerful purpose or benefit for practicing productive thoughts.

Which is better for your physical body — unhealthy, destructive thoughts or loving, caring, compassionate thoughts? The answer seems obvious. If you would like more in depth knowledge about attitudes and their effect on the physical body in very specific ways then read a book I wrote called Permanent Healing. Permanent Healing contains an in depth glossary of hundreds of physical dis-orders and dis-eases and the way they each alter specific areas of the physical body in specific ways.

When gratitude is expressed the giver realizes he or she is in control of life again. You are no longer a victim of circumstances. Instead, you are a creator of your life and you learn and grow from all you draw to you. All experiences are for your learning. Why would or does anyone refuse the learning? There are two reasons for refusing the learning: fear and ignorance. Usually the answer is fear.

Fear controls most people's lives in one way or another. By focusing on love, LIGHT, and truth and by desiring to learn and grow, one is able to overcome fear. For fear is of the darkness and LIGHT always dispels darkness.

Gratitude benefits you.

Gratitude benefits the one giving gratitude.

Purpose is personal benefit. Therefore, gratitude gives more purpose to one's life.

Gratitude brings you into the present where you can enjoy the benefits of life. For only in the present can you fulfill your purpose.

The giver of gratitude is more capable of receiving the purpose of life.

In a likewise manner the one who forgives also updates the brain and is more capable of effectively using the conscious mind. One who forgives is also more capable of fulfilling the purpose of life.

Life is designed to be lived in the present moment. Only by being fully invested in the present can one reap the full benefits of the experiences and purpose of one's life. Forgiveness and gratitude are powerful tools for more fully moving one's consciousness and attention into the present moment.

Thought to remember:
I give thanks.

What to do:

1. State out loud

    I forgive <u>name of person</u>.

2. Next state out loud

    I give gratitude for <u>name of same person</u>.

    Do this day after day until you gain peace and freedom within your own Self concerning this person, situation, or circumstance.

Chapter 9
Imagination, Choice and Purpose

1. Imagination is necessary to imagine a purpose.
2. Imagination is necessary to create.
3. Imagination is necessary to create an idea.
4. Ideas form the basis and are the origination point of any creation.

Choosing and creating a higher purpose is the way or technology for upgrading one's consciousness.

People who fulfill their purpose in life constantly upgrade their thoughts, attitudes, and mental images. This upgrading process leads to great initiations and transformations in consciousness.

How can one create a purpose for an activity when there doesn't seem to be any desire to perform that activity, effort or work?

The answer is choice. You choose. You choose to perform an action even if it does not have or contain the sensory gratification you crave.

There are two great mental powers that each person has available to use. These two great powers are:

1. **Imaging**
2. **Choosing**

More people are familiar with the term *imaging* in its alternate form *imagination*. However, the word imagination is sometimes used to mean illusion as in the phrase, "it's all in your imagination" or "you just imagined that."

Therefore, I use the root form of imagination to indicate one who chooses to create mental images. These mental images form the basis of all creation. In other words, thought is cause. Everything begins with a thought.

In order to create a productive thought one must choose a thought that one can create. Since most people think mostly the same thoughts each day, they create little that is new or that dramatically improves their station in life.

Imagination and choice are the keys to dramatically improving one's position, station or prosperity in life.

It is easy to say, "choose a different thought." It is <u>less</u> easy to do so. Many great inventions in the world came after months or years of thoughtful deliberation and creative dreaming — thinking on the part of the individual.

WILL

Once a person begins to identify his or her purpose in life then the will can be employed effectively. Until the purpose is discerned, the use of the will is scattered, distracted, wasted or only partially used.

The will can be employed effectively to accomplish physical goals. A physical goal by itself is not enough to feed the soul because it is temporary.

The will is a series of choices or decisions toward a goal or ideal.

What is the difference between a goal and an ideal?

A goal is what one wants to do.
An ideal is what one wants to be or become.

Goals are mental images usually of physical things one wants to achieve.

To come to know Self and one's purpose in life one must have more than goals, one must create and have an ideal for the Self.

Ideals are of the nature of ideas.

The highest ideal is en-LIGHT-en-ment. Each of us, each person, was created as an individual unit of LIGHT called I AM. The LIGHT I am describing here is more than physical light. Our essence as LIGHT is awareness. Whether you call each individual a person, a soul, or a spirit, such a one is in fact a being whose essence is LIGHT. This LIGHT is awareness and this being of LIGHT is "I AM".

This is why the words, "Man, know thyself" were placed above the doorways of the great temples of learning of antiquity.

The word man comes from the Sanskrit word *manu* and means thinker. Therefore, the statement above the doorways of these great schools of learning meant or indicated that each thinker, each reasoner, is to discipline the mind in order to know the Self as a being of LIGHT, an enlightened being.

In order to successfully exercise the will there needs to be purpose with the goal. Purpose is personal benefit. As one creates a purpose on a daily basis one comes to a greater understanding of purpose. As one practices purpose on a small scale or daily basis one comes to know the larger purpose and a purpose on a greater scale. As one's purpose expands this translates into a greater awareness of the purpose of life.

Reasoning helps build will because one can learn from the results of choices. Reasoning is made up of the three factors of memory, attention and imagination. It is the imagination that must be employed effectively in order for a greater purpose to be formulated.

People often lack purpose or a strong enough purpose to motivate them to quicken their growth as a soul or LIGHT being. Therefore, I teach purpose to students on a regular basis.

People have difficulty finishing what they have begun. It requires determination to complete what has been initiated. Lasting determination derives from ideal and purpose. Ideal and purpose produce a sustainable will that can be employed to achieve almost anything.

Purpose is the benefit one receives from anything done, any activity. When one has a strong purpose for giving then that purpose does not depend on how what one gives is received. We are here on Earth, in a physical body, to learn how to give and receive completely. It is in giving and receiving that we are afforded the opportunity to learn, grow and advance our consciousness.

A good exercise to practice every day is to ask yourself out loud, "What is my purpose?" for every activity done during the day.

Before long you will begin to notice the many things you do throughout the day that are entirely from habit or old memories stored in the brain. Then you will have the awareness to choose a purpose in areas and ways that you were not even aware of before.

Thought to remember:

The mind must be more fully engaged in order to understand purpose, and that means making choices.

What to do:

Imagine a great purpose for yourself each day.

Chapter 10
The conscious ego and Purpose

The ego's part in fulfillment of the life's purpose

The conscious ego is the motivator for the conscious mind. The conscious ego is the distorted way your individuality, your I AM, appears in the conscious mind. The conscious ego motivates you to survive. Along with the conscious mind, the conscious ego motivates you to solve problems.

The difficulty with the conscious ego arises due to the fact that being associated with the conscious mind it tends to function mostly at a physical level. This means that its motivations are often physical.

During the process of growing to understand and fulfill one's purpose it may seem at times as if the ego is changing or dying. This is because the conscious ego is evolving into higher awareness of Self as I AM.

The History of Human Beings on Earth and its Relationship to One's Life Purpose

In the early days of the development of life forms on planet Earth various life forms developed. One of these life forms was mammals. Out of mammals developed humanoid mammals.

These humanoid mammals developed a greater brain capacity for their size than most of the other animals around them.

Then through some outside influence they began to evolve even more. They walked upright, had opposable thumbs for grasping and generally became smarter.

Then conscious beings from the inner levels of Mind, such as the Subconscious Mind, began to inhabit these animal men or humanoid type bodies. This is still what is going on in the present. Presently we inhabit a physical, highly intelligent, but not enlightened physical body.

This physical body has a sort of rudimentary sort of intelligence. Therefore, it seeks to control. Its method is to invent problems and to then keep the thoughts busy trying to solve those problems.

When the soul or subconscious mind succumbs to these physical thoughts, the Real Self becomes entrapped in a physical body and engrossed in the experiences of the senses. When this occurs you think you are the physical body. This is an illusion. This is a falsity for you are not the physical body. The physical body is a vehicle that the Real Self called I AM inhabits.

People who develop, understand, and fulfill their life's purpose have tapped into and discovered who they really are as an immortal I AM.

What we call human beings are essentially I AM's entrapped in physical bodies.

It is the animal body and brain consciousness in which we were raised that leads us to war and conflict. In contrast, I AM has no conflict. I AM exists in the peace of a still mind and thus knows pure consciousness. Those that have attained this state have achieved Buddha consciousness, Christ consciousness, Zarathustra consciousness and cosmic consciousness.

The busy mind will never give one enlightenment because those thoughts are of the physical brain and its attendant conscious mind.

Purpose is found in the still mind. The reason purpose is found in the still mind is that true and deep purpose is found in the depths of one's being.

There exists purpose in one's waking conscious mind.
There exists purpose in subconscious mind.
There exists purpose in superconscious mind.
The still mind enables one to experience purpose on
 all levels of one's being.

You are a valuable and important person. Purpose causes one to realize Self value because purpose is personal benefit. Having purpose is the ability to image a benefit in the activity of experience. To gain the benefit one must be willing to receive the benefit.

In order to receive the benefit of any experience sometimes change is required. Sometimes I say to my students, "When all else fails, change!"

To change means to surrender the conscious ego and be willing to open up and receive in a way one was not willing to previously. Change may also require one to stretch and reach beyond previously accepted limitations.

The Conscious Ego and Purpose

To choose a productive thought is valuable. To make a productive thought a part of one's consciousness requires repeating the thought over and over out loud. In addition one needs to find or create ways to apply the productive thought each day.

When saying a positive affirmation, give it full attention. Repetition and the quality of attention determine how well, how quickly and how deeply the greater truth sinks into one's consciousness. Repetition and full attention ensure that the new, greater thought will take hold inside the Self.

To learn a new and greater truth it is important to use as many of the five physical senses as possible. This is why causing self to have new experiences that put one in the heart of the learning are invaluable.

Brain — memory — past
Mind — imagination — future
Consciousness — attention — present

When speaking the greater truth out loud the sense of hearing is employed.

Reading the greater truth out loud employs both the sense of hearing and sight. The sense of touch is also involved because when reading out loud, one's lips are moving.

To create a higher purpose requires going beyond brain memory to use the mind aggressively. To receive a greater truth into the self requires using the mind receptively.

To receive one's purpose from the inner or subconscious mind into the outer, conscious mind requires a disciplined mind, a still mind and control of one's attention.

Which do you prefer, stimulation or motivation?

Stimulation comes from the outer, physical, sensory environment. Stimulation is temporary and can cause temporary movement or motivation.

Permanent and lasting motivation comes from within and is caused by developing purpose.

The limitation of stimulation is that it is temporary.

Think about the stimulus of eating your favorite food. Think about a time when you have eaten that food until you did not want to eat it anymore. Think about how long it was before you ate that food again.

Think about smelling a rose. The first time it smells really good. As you continue smelling it you notice you can't smell it as well anymore. By the third or fourth or tenth time you can't smell the rose very much or you do not want to smell the rose.

Think about watching a beautiful sunset. How many days in a row do you want to see a sunset? How many hours a day do you want to watch sunsets?

The greatest benefit, and therefore purpose, is the universal truths that you add to yourself permanently.

The five sense receptors are receiving stations or receiving mechanisms designed to receive information or experience from the physical world around us.

To receive means the individual has the opportunity to add something to the Self.

So give up the idea that time and lasting security comes from your old ideas and old memory thoughts.

True and lasting security is in the stillness of the mind. All creation proceeds from this.

Growth in awareness, understanding and consciousness is a process of receiving greater truth into the Self.

1. **Truth that is given attention is retrievable as memory from the brain and is stored in the brain.**
2. **Truth that is practiced and applied in the life is stored in the heart and in the conscious mind.**
3. **Truth that is then taught to others is stored as permanent understanding in one's subconscious mind.**

The surrendered ego is very important in this process. An egotistical person thinks he or she knows it all. If you already know it all, how is it possible to receive more? What is the motivation to even listen to another?

To listen to another is to accept the truth that there is more to learn and you need to learn it. In the process you realize you have more to give also.

The conscious ego is very insecure. So when you surrender your conscious ego you surrender insecurity.

The conscious ego is the motivator of Self. Yet purpose also provides motivation. How can both the conscious ego and purpose be the motivator? The answer is the conscious ego will motivate you to achieve physical goals, while purpose will motivate you to achieve and receive permanent and lasting fulfillment, peace and the achievement of ideals.

Purpose provides the motivation to discipline the conscious mind and surrender the conscious ego.

One can either imagine a purpose for the Self and visualize it or one can receive a purpose from a teacher. Either way the purpose needs to be internalized.

An honest ego is motivated to learn, grow, and change the Self. A dishonest conscious ego is not.

Purpose in conjunction with an honest ego propels or moves one toward the ideal of enlightenment and achieving one's full potential.

An honest ego aligns with Universal Law, Universal Truth and greater connectedness with all of creation.

The honest conscious ego moves forward to alignment with I AM, which is the Real you.

The one who has a strong ideal is willing to sacrifice one's limitations.

Purpose is not the reason for doing something. One can have a reason for doing something yet find that action does not benefit the Self.

Neither is purpose defined as the way you will be different by accomplishing a goal.

People accomplish goals all the time yet do not change much from this.

Purpose is personal benefit. Therefore, purpose is what you will permanently add to your whole Self while in the process of moving toward a goal or achieving and becoming your ideal.

Imagination is vitally important in order to achieve your ideal Self and realize your greatest aspirations.

People with weak imaginations tend to function mostly from memory. They then only re-create what they have experienced in the past.

People that understand the power of thought wield the imaginative faculty. The person who has a strong image of the ideal Self she desires to become is willing to sacrifice her limitations.

People that function mostly from memory of the past see little benefit in changing because their so called security is based upon what they have seen, done or experienced in the past.

Yet the past cannot give anyone enlightenment. The past does not make anyone a whole functioning Self. The past does not enable you to go beyond limitations. **Only the attention given to the present situation in order to create a better future will fulfill the purpose of life.**

How many people are willing to sacrifice their limitations? Most people have thought of something terrible happening associated with sacrifice.

Or I could ask, "How many people are willing to surrender their limitations?" Most people do not want to surrender either.

Yet limitations must be changed or transformed into

strengths. Consciousness must expand if the individual is to achieve his or her true destiny.

To sacrifice is to transform a lower energy or thought to a higher energy or thought.

To surrender is to stop fighting and to stop making war. To surrender is to receive and accept what your higher Self, your inner Self, your Superconscious Self has to offer you.

The lower conscious mind must receive what the higher Subconscious mind and Superconscious mind have to offer in order to fulfill the purpose of life which includes your individual purpose.

A strong ideal of what one wants to become creates a willingness to sacrifice one's limitations.

When thinking of sacrifice most people conjure up an image of being burned on a funeral pyre or facing oblivion.

The great unspoken fear that many and perhaps most people have is the fear of annihilation, death or obliteration. This is the fear of ceasing to exist.

There is another type of physical sacrifice that people sometimes think of. This is the act of sacrificing yourself for a higher cause such as your country. Soldiers may die on the battlefield to protect their country. Dying for another may be the ultimate physical sacrifice.

Concerning fulfilling one's purpose, the old outworn concepts and limited or habitual thinking must be sacrificed to a higher consciousness and greater wisdom. This is a sacrifice of the mind and its limiting mental attitudes.

A reasoner creates purpose. The purpose of experiences is to give the one experiencing benefits.

What is the greatest benefit?

The fulfillment of one's life purpose.

The mind needs to be trained to either think a thought or to be still. To be still is to have no thoughts in your mind.

In this way the mind is like a computer. For computers function on binary code. A binary code is a two digit code such as 0,1. In computers the two numbers of zero and one are given as on and off. Off can indicate zero and on can indicate one.

The mind accomplishes the same thing when it chooses to either think a thought or to have no thought.

An undisciplined mind which is incessantly busy while habitually thinking many thoughts is never able to be high powered. It is never able to make full use of the binary system of calculating which powers the world's supercomputers.

Thus a busy, restless mind is not only less powerful than a disciplined mind, the busy mind is very weak.

The disciplined mind represents a quantum leap over an undisciplined mind. The more disciplined the mind becomes, the more quantum leaps forward in consciousness, reasoning and awareness the individual accomplishes.

This is why the accomplishments of some unique people seem to be the work of a superman or 100 people. It is the power of a disciplined mind.

Then the conscious ego becomes surrendered, the conscious mind becomes surrendered, the brain becomes surrendered and the individual lives in a state of freedom of choice. No longer is the Self bound to the past or to the future. Rather, the Self exists in the eternal present, where all choices, all opportunities become available. The individual exists in a state of potentiality where creation and the possibility of creation exits in each moment.

Who can learn in the past?
No one.

Who can create in the past?
No one.
The power is in the present moment.

It is possible to review one's memories of the past and decide if they are applicable to the present. It is possible to apply the lessons of the past to the present. Yet the application, the creation, is always in the present, the eternal now.

Now is the time to learn.
Now is the time to reason.
Now is the time to still the mind.
Now is the time to expand one's consciousness.

To surrender to the present moment is to make oneself fully capable of receiving the present experience. The only way one can learn is to receive the present experience.

The ego, which likes to motivate one to do things, will not like this idea of surrender. To surrender is to receive the learning. The conscious ego wants to be aggressive.

Thought to remember:
    The ego is the motivator in physical waking life.
    To gain enlightenment, the conscious ego has to die or be replaced with I AM.

What to do:
    Still your mind and listen, over and over again.

Chapter 11
My discoveries of the brain, the mind and purpose

The vast majority of people live their lives for the temporary. Many do not focus on learning in life at all. They just focus on what gives them temporary sense pleasure. Those that do focus on temporary learning feed more and more information into the brain yet fail to make real, lasting, growth-filled changes in the whole Self and the whole mind.

It requires a big shift in thinking, a big shift in consciousness, to come to know the difference between the brain and the mind. Even greater effort and wisdom is needed to integrate the understanding and willful, directed use of the mind into one's consciousness and life.

Sometimes decisions based upon using the whole mind and knowing the whole Self seem to run counter to the desire for sensory experience or information fed into the brain.

The key to remember is: The mind is the vehicle one uses to build permanent understandings.

The brain is a physical organ designed to receive sensory experiences for effective functioning in daily experience.

The brain stores memories of the past. The mind creates images of the future. Consciousness exists in the present.

In order to come to know one's individual purpose in life, one must image, visualize and create purpose for everything in one's life. In other words, the practice of having and creating purpose for everything you do must become second nature.

Developing purpose must become integrated into one's consciousness in order to develop the means to receive and know one's purpose in life.

The purpose of a lifetime is received from subconscious mind. Purpose is received into the conscious mind from the subconscious mind.

Therefore, create and have a purpose for listening. Create and have a purpose for the words you speak. Words are to be used to convey one's thoughts. Words convey thoughts. Words that are misused in an attempt to mislead or obfuscate or cover up one's real thoughts is dishonesty.

Dishonesty does not add to one's soul growth. Dishonesty retards and detracts from one's soul growth and spiritual development. Have an open mind and listen to others with the purpose of adding to the Self.

You can never move forward by avoiding that which you need to learn.

Four keys for gaining the essence of the learning in every experience.

1. Separate
2. Identify
3. Admit
4. Connect

The true nature of reality is connectedness. Since the true nature of reality is connectedness these "four keys for gaining the essence of learning" must fit in with and apply to creating greater connectedness.

1. The first key is for the individual to be able to separate the facts of the experience.

The facts will always relate to the person that is investigating himself or herself. The facts will always involve one's thoughts, for we create our life by our thoughts.

Thought is Cause.

The statement "Thought is Cause" is a Universal Truth.

Universal Truths explain Universal Laws. Universal Laws govern the Universe in the sense that they provide the framework and structure for creation in both the physical universe and the Universal, Subconscious Mind.

The statement "Thought is Cause" indicates that we create our own life. Our thoughts determine our decisions and our decisions determine the outcome of our life.

Decisions determine will power, determination, choosing truth, love, compassion, caring, harmony, discipline and a host of other good and productive qualities.

Decisions can also be unproductive and out of alignment with Universal Truth and Universal Law. These kinds of decisions always bring pain and sorrow in their wake both for the perpetrator and for the people around such a one.

Therefore, the first key in gaining the essence of learning is to separate out everything you have thought, said or done that put you in the present situation.

The purpose or benefit of separating out all the facts is so you can learn and become more connected. When the facts and details have been separated out then you are ready to progress to the next stage of understanding your purpose.

2. The next stage or step is called "Identify."

Identifying is the step of examining and looking at the facts of a situation or experience in your life and identifying all the details of that experience.

The first stage called "separate" brings the general experience to your awareness. In the first stage you can separate out this one particular experience from all other experiences. It is the process of separation that allows you to identify the separate, individual parts of any situation and circumstance.

By separating out one's own thoughts you can identify which thought or thoughts lead to the present situation or circumstance, be it pleasurable or painful.

By identifying the various parts or aspects of an experience one can admit the thoughts and decisions one had that produced this experience.

3. The third step is to admit.

Sometimes one's thoughts and their attendant choices put the Self in a situation or experience created by others. By separating, identifying and admitting your thoughts, you can perceive how your choices and decisions put you in the current situation.

Admitting your part in creating your life and any part of your life is empowering. It enables you to admit you are the Creator of your life. Identifying and admitting the way you create your life enables the recognition that you can change or improve your life for the better.

Most everyone, given the choice, would like to see improvement in themselves and their life. Most people would like to better themselves. The keys are to learn how you created your life the way it is and how to create your life to be the way you desire.

Blame gives the person practicing blame no power. Blame is a false sense of power. The person placing blame is in effect saying someone else has the power in my life. Someone else controls my life.

In contrast to blame, purpose provides personal benefit to the individual. In so doing, purpose imparts power, control and authority.

Blame is the refusal to admit the power of your own thoughts. You create your thoughts and choices based upon thoughts, and choices are the way you create your life. Therefore, thoughts and choices are what give or impart the power to create. Blame is a refusal to admit this power.

Choices are based upon thought. Imagination gives each person the opportunity to move ahead with thought. What we image, visualize or think is the basis for our choices.

Choices repeated toward an ideal or goal can build will power.

Will and imagination are two powerful keys for knowing Self and for knowing one's purpose in life.

Admitting one's part and role in creating one's current situations and circumstances aligns one with the true nature of reality which is connectedness. Connectedness is the 4th stage of creating change and fulfilling one's life purpose.

4. The fourth step or stage is called Connect.

Separating, identifying, and admitting one's thoughts and actions prepares the Self to connect with the true nature of reality which is connectedness.

In truth, each person, each individual is already connected even if it is not in his or her consciousness.

Therefore, this fourth step is a function of gaining the awareness of the true nature of reality. It comes from practicing the first three steps of separating, identifying and admitting.

In order to fulfill one's true purpose in life, one's purpose must be aligned with the Universal Laws and Universal Truths of Connectedness.

Connectedness is what we are all striving for whether realized or not. We experience the connectedness of family, of friends, of community, of nation and of the world. Yet there always seems to be that part of us that is not connected or fully connected with those we meet.

The key is to connect all aspects of Self together.

This is done by disciplining the mind until one's thoughts are quieted and the mind becomes still.

Then the mind enters a state or condition of no thought. When no thought is present then the Self experiences the connected and pure consciousness that pervades everything and connects everything.

No longer are you the weak, puny, isolated, lonely person trying to survive. Instead you become the being connected with all the resources and power of the universe.

Connectedness is the true nature of reality. When the mind is still, Self may experience this as love, LIGHT, radiance, wholeness, bliss, joy or peace or all of these.

Living the connected consciousness is to be alive. It is a thousand or a million times more alive than a thought-filled mind. This is because the peaceful, still mind aligns and identifies with the true nature of reality which is connectedness.

The busy, thought-filled mind is engrossed in the illusion of separateness. Therefore, it cannot function properly. Since it can only function in extremes, it experiences pleasure and pain. Often the busy mind experiences pain and suffering. This pain and suffering occurs because the person is living the life based upon mistaken ideas and mistaken perceptions. Busy, disconnected minds think the physical life is permanent and lasting when it is actually temporary.

Busy, physically thinking brains believe little if anything exists beyond physical life. This is untrue. The greater reality exists beyond the conscious mind and physical existence.

Beyond the world of the five senses lies the world of perception, of LIGHT, of love, of awareness, of peace, of connectedness and of reality.

As long as the mind, brain and attention are caught up in these thoughts concerning sensory experiences there will be little ability to experience the higher consciousness.

The higher consciousness contains the greatest benefits for it is the source point for all creation and all growth in awareness.

Purpose is never negative, in the sense that purpose never takes away. Purpose is never a matter of not doing something just as will is never a matter of not choosing to do something.

All the really productive and valuable qualities and understandings of life are a process of adding to what one already has built in the Self.

Since purpose is choosing what one wants to add to the Self, purpose is always positive.

A purpose may be to learn how to communicate better or to become more open, honest, friendly or caring. A purpose may be to gain, build or learn fortitude, commitment, inner strength, greater love, or to achieve one's full potential and purpose in life.

Purpose never takes from who you are. Purpose always adds to who you are and your awareness of who you are.

You actually don't choose not to do something. To choose not to do something is to actually chose to move your attention from one place to another.

For example, if you choose not to wash the dishes you are actually choosing to do something else such as mop the floor or read a book.

So it is with purpose. Purpose is never a negative. There is never a not associated with purpose.

Purpose gives the opportunity to add to yourself and your consciousness.

Purpose provides desire that comes from inside the Self.

The outer environment provides sensory stimulus from which outer desires are formed.

Purpose is personal benefit. As one grows in consciousness and awareness there is the greater realization that helping others benefits the Self. All greater and prosperous countries and communities recognize this.

The five physical senses of sight, hearing, smell, taste and touch give the false illusion that everything is separate.

For example, a person may think "I am separate from that table because I am separated by distance." The truth is everything and everyone is connected.

Quantum physics posits that the experimenter affects the experience. This has been verified over and over. This is, in effect, saying we are all connected.

Therefore, the most powerful purposes are those that connect. These connections can be with others, they can be with our inner Self, they can be with all creation or with LIGHT or Love or Truth.

One who has a still mind can perceive the connectedness of people, places and things. One who has a still mind will perceive the connections between a past thought and a present circumstance.

As the still mind is made more and more one's consciousness the Self realizes and experiences connectedness as real.

Some people are afraid of having a still mind. I have found that even after years of practicing concentration and meditation, some people fear or do not see the value of a still mind. So now I teach the purpose, which is the personal benefits, of having a still mind.

This makes all the difference in the world when a student understands the benefits of a still mind. Often people think they can accomplish more in a day by thinking more thoughts and thinking thoughts faster. After all if you are already thinking thoughts all day long, all the time, and you believe thinking more thoughts makes you more effective, then your mind has to race faster in order to think more thoughts than the day before and thereby be more effective.

The previous sentence may seem rather long yet it serves to illustrate the point of many people's thinking.

Therefore, I educate people as to the fact that a still mind which from time to time thinks thoughts, is more effective than a busy mind with lots of thoughts.

Purpose and Benefits of a Still Mind

1. Peace
2. Greater Health
3. More effective reasoning
4. Alignment with the true nature of reality
5. Perception beyond the illusions of sensory engrossment
6. Less headaches
7. Less worry, guilt, fear, doubt, anger, hatred, resentment and other negative thinking that are limitations in consciousness.
8. Greater Self value and Self respect
9. A strong mind
10. A strong will

11. A powerful and productive imagination.
12. Aligns conscious and subconscious minds to know the purpose of one's life
13. Improved listening ability
14. Increased receptivity
15. Greater mental discipline
16. Food no longer controls you
17. Imparts the freedom to create
18. Make the thoughts you choose more sensible
19. A recognition of a continuum of consciousness
20. Awareness of who you are
21. Greater inner strength
22. Greater control of your physical body
23. Makes all diets work better
24. Makes all food work better
25. Imparts a greater ability to give love
26. Imparts a greater ability to receive love.
27. Greater fulfillment of goals, ideals, and purposes
28. Greater joy and bliss
29. Greater peace of mind
30. Fulfillment

Every negative or destructive thought about oneself will limit and restrict you in your work towards Self knowing because they are of the brain. Negative thoughts about the Self have been learned this lifetime and stored as memory in the brain.

The brain cannot make you enlightened.

Only the disciplined, purposeful, productive use of the mind in alignment with Universal Law and Universal Truth will cause any individual to become enlightened.

Negative thoughts about the Self stored in the brain have been received by the conscious mind. They will continue to be practiced by the brain and influence the conscious mind until one chooses to discipline the conscious mind to think positively.

Brain pathways, habits, attitudes, personality and ways of thinking stored as memory in the brain exist for our learning. They are by their very nature limited.

Consciousness does not expand in the brain. Consciousness expands throughout all of Mind when the individual mind is still.

Therefore, the mind must be directed in order to reprogram the brain. The brain must be reprogrammed or redesigned or remade in order to be in alignment with Universal Laws and Universal Truth. Then the brain can be lit up or filled with the LIGHT of awareness.

Brain pathways are not permanent and lasting. They are meant to be for the soul, the inner or Real Self's learning concerning Self as a Creator.

Parents give us the first brain images that we receive.

We choose our parents for the learning they give us early in life. We form a personality around this early training. As we mature we either live in the brain maintaining the same personality all our lives or we listen to and follow our soul urge.

When we listen to and follow our soul urge we are reborn in the sense of developing a whole new and higher consciousness. This higher consciousness makes of us a different, a more enlightened being, that neither accepts nor identifies with the old, limited, ways of thinking.

The Higher Consciousness is built first upon a still mind. Then the thoughts that are created in the mind are of the highest caliber.

The highest caliber, the most enlightened, thoughts are those that are filled with Love, LIGHT, and Truth.

The more enlightened one becomes the less thoughts one thinks.

The average person, engrossed in the senses, has a busy mind filled with thoughts in rapid fire motion.

The first step to gaining awareness and knowledge of the Self, and therefore one's purpose, is to learn to gain the ability to choose your thoughts.

You may think, "But I do choose my thoughts every day!" To which I reply, "If you are unaware of all or some of your thoughts then you are not choosing those thoughts. In addition any habitual thoughts you have are not being consciously chosen."

Thought to Remember:
    Use the brain for memory.
    Use the mind for imagination.
    Use the attention for awareness.

What to do:
    Be in the present moment.

Chapter 12
Desires and Purpose

Accessing One's Purpose Through Desire

Desire is another portal or opening to access and discover your purpose in life.

Desires start out as urges for physical things such as the desire for a car, a job or new clothes. These desires progress to an urge for friendships, love and a sense of belonging.

For some these desires progress to an urge, a real need, to know the purpose of life. For these ones the question arises, "Doesn't life have more meaning than just sensory gratification? Doesn't life have more meaning than just a few friends, some sense pleasure, and a vague sense of loneliness and separation?"

From this the desire evolves to a longing to know the purpose of life, the real nature of the Self and what exists beyond the physical sensory world.

Because the mind is the vehicle or tool of the Self, it will respond to intelligent direction. Therefore, when a truth seeking person earnestly sends out a mental call for help and desires to know the truth, the mind responds. The person begins to notice things that went unnoticed before such as a lecture, a group meeting or a class that might answer some of one's questions.

You may experience a so-called chance meeting with someone who can provide you with answers. You may find your teacher. It is all predicated on listening to your inner voice and responding.

Too many people are sad and unfulfilled in life because they have never lived their life's purpose. And the reason this life's purpose remains unfulfilled is because the person stops paying attention to the inner Self, the subconscious mind, and the superconscious mind. The reason the person stops listening to the inner Self is the attention becomes engrossed and attached to sensory experiences and memories of these.

Instead of being in the present moment, most people have most of their attention in past memories or future worries. To the extent the attention is in the present, it is due to physical sensory experiences such as food, sex, buying new things, or seeing new things.

Rare is the person who has the capability to direct the mind with will and choice at any time. Rarer still is the evolved one who can still the mind at will.

In the still mind one receives inspiration from the subconscious mind. This is using the power of the subconscious mind.

When the still mind is practiced and experienced regularly and consistently, one begins to experience superconscious inspiration and awareness. The LIGHT of one's inner Self begins to reveal itself in one's outer countenance. Life becomes a process of unfoldment.

Once you begin this process of unfoldment into truth, love and LIGHT the motivation increases with each truth you receive. Desire for more and greater truth quickens and grows. With each step forward in fulfillment of the purpose, one's commitment to fulfilling that purpose increases.

Once you have tasted the higher truth, the Universal Truths, the high knowledge and the greater awareness, the thirst for more understandings quickens. In this way the motivation to know and fulfill one's purpose strengthens and is enhanced.

As greater awareness of the purpose of life enters, give it out through your words. When speaking newly found truth you will hear your own truth filled words. In this way the higher truth, the higher purpose, becomes firmly built in the conscious mind.

Truth, to be understood, must be received through the five senses in order that greater truth may be received in through the higher mind.

People that apply mental discipline in the life have the capability of increasing fulfillment of their purpose 10 fold or 100 fold. This is because most people think 90 to 95 percent of the same thoughts each day. In other words, most of the thoughts in people's heads are memory thoughts. The difficulty with this is that in order to learn, grow and succeed in life, attention and imagination must also be employed.

To live in one's memory is to relive the past over and over again. It is a trap that keeps one locked in the past. Great inventors, creators, and discoverers use imagination to a high degree and thus do not become locked in the past.

There are three parts to reasoning called memory, attention and imagination. When a person fails to make use of imagination and relies too much on memory there is a tendency to get trapped in logic.

What is the difference between logic and reasoning? Reasoning employs memory, attention and imagination while logic relies for the most part only on memory and attention.

To fulfill and understand one's purpose to a greater degree than before the present, one must think different thoughts.

In addition to thinking different thoughts which lead to different choices, one must still the mind and thoughts more often. It is necessary to still the thoughts because then the waking conscious mind may receive awareness of life's purpose from the subconscious mind.

Thought to Remember:

    Cause physical desires to evolve and strengthen your need to know the Self.

What to do:

    Fulfill one outer desire each day.

    Fulfill one inner desire each day.

Chapter 13
Activity, Experience and Purpose

There is no replacement for experience.

You can read book after book on riding a bicycle, yet you will not know how to ride a bicycle until you actually get on and practice.

The same holds true for understanding the purpose of life. It is imperative that the one desiring greater purpose in the life make choices that produce the activity and effort needed to create the experiences one needs to learn the lessons of the life.

In other words, you won't become enlightened sitting in meditation all day long. Nor will you understand your purpose by just sitting around thinking about it. Meditation can help you discover purpose when you apply your meditation born awareness to every experience in your life.

Look at your life. Are you doing the same activity day after day, week after week, month after month, year after year? Are you always around the same people? Or does your experience change over time? If your mind is growing, if your awareness is growing, if your consciousness is growing then your experiences will change.

In order to fulfill your life's purpose, you are going to receive more knowledge, awareness, understanding and wisdom. To receive these you will have to give to others more. You will need to place yourself in a position of helpfulness. You may decide to teach others whatever you know about the Universal Truths of Life.

For example, as I learn more about the purpose of life I teach this to others. I have been doing so for over a quarter of a century.

I have taught students concentration, meditation, visualization, memory, listening, self discipline, self value, dream interpretation, Universal Laws and Universal Truths, goal creating, imaging, will power and many, many more tools for development of the mind and self awareness.

As I have taught these to others, I have grown in Self awareness. I have gained greater understandings of the purpose of life and how I may fulfill it.

Teaching others is an activity I choose. Teaching others is an experience I would not have if I did not choose to give.

It is okay to be uncomfortable in a new experience. Most people tend to avoid experiences they are not comfortable with.

However, successful people, that is people that achieve great things in life, are the ones that don't allow comfort or discomfort to be the focal point of any choice they make.

Instead, people that achieve their purpose in life have clearly imaged goals and ideals and act upon them regardless of the ease or difficulty with which they are achieved. Anything worth achieving always requires effort. It is in stretching and reaching that we grow. We must stretch not only our bodies but also our minds and our emotions.

People must come out of their shell if they are to grow. The shell is one's own Self created limitations.

Think of a child, an infant. Does a baby, a child, worry about being uncomfortable when learning to talk, crawl or walk. Of course not. An infant sees adults speaking and imitates them. A child sees adults walking and imitates them. Most of the time the child has fun learning to walk and talk.

It is a stretch and a reach for the child to walk. This is a good model for adults to remember. Discovering your purpose in life and fulfilling it is a reach and a stretch. Therefore, enjoy the learning, enjoy the new experience, value the opportunity to reach, grow and learn something new.

A recent study found that the number one fear of Americans was the fear of public speaking. The fear of public speaking ranked even higher than the fear of death! As I often tell my students, the way to get over the fear of giving lectures is to give lectures. The way to get over the fear of teaching is to teach. The way to get over the fear of swimming is to get in the water and practice swimming.

In other words, avoidance of the learning opportunities available gives you nothing.

If you don't know your next step in life and are unsatisfied with where you are, then stop thinking the same old things and doing the same old things.

Remember, nobody ever got enlightened by themselves. Everyone needs help. No man (thinker) or wo-man (extension of the thinker) is an island. We are here on this green and blue Earth to aid each other to fulfill that Divine Plan of enlightenment. We are here to fulfill our purpose. We need each other to fulfill our purpose. We need to share, give and receive of our highest thoughts, our deepest feeling, our loftiest ideal and our greatest experiences with each other.

We are here to fulfill our purpose through creating together. To create together we must have activity, which is to produce a physical experience together.

To create is not just to be in an experience. To create is to produce an experience with others through our effort and actions. This is the productive use of activity.

Some people are doers. They get things done. Other people wonder what just happened.

Often, doers need to learn about themselves and how to fulfill their purpose through what they are doing. Just because you can get physical things done doesn't mean you understand purpose or how to fulfill your purpose.

Sometimes people get burned out on their work. They think they have to take time off from work. This may be because they have learned everything they can learn from the activity they are doing at the present time.

I remember a time in college when I got to a similar point or place within myself. I remember thinking very clearly, "I've learned everything I can learn at this university." That was the best way I knew how to express what I was experiencing at the time.

As time went by and I grew in awareness, I learned how to better express or explain what I meant by that statement. What I meant and was experiencing was a need for a different kind of learning, a different kind of activity. What I had received in my four years of undergraduate work plus one year of graduate level coursework was a lot of information for my brain. I read a lot of books and took a lot of notes and a lot of tests.

Something was missing when I enrolled in the Master's program. I thought I would become more fulfilled. As part of my masters work for a degree in Agricultural Economics I traveled to Peru, South America where I lived for four months while I collected data for my master's thesis.

I found this experience to be stimulating and fulfilling because it provided me with a kind of experience I had never had. I spoke a foreign language. I ate different foods. I lived in a different climate. I was collecting data instead of memorizing information for a test. I was meeting new people. I visited ancient holy sites of the Incas and pre-Incas such as Machu-Picchu, Cuzco, Sachsawaman, and Lake Titicaca.

Yet when I returned to Columbia, Missouri the first thing I did was look for alternative ways of learning and ways I could develop my mind such as meditation, visualization and concentration.

Sometimes you've learned everything you can learn from the old activity and it is time to do something new.

The day-to-day practice of purpose

It is always the little things, the little steps, that lead to the big steps. That is why I have included this chapter about the day to day practice of purpose.

Purpose is not attached to other people. It is attached or connected to the Self and the way the Self can be made better. In other words, other people do not fulfill your purpose in life. You fulfill your purpose in life through your experiences with others.

Fulfillment of one's highest purpose is enlightenment.

Since enlightenment is beyond the conscious mind, one must still the thoughts in the conscious mind in order to perceive the enlightenment that is behind and beyond the conscious mind.

The still mind has no conscious thoughts and is therefore free to receive the higher knowledge, wisdom and enlightenment from superconscious mind and I AM.

If the purpose of life is not the creation of thoughts

and

> **the purpose of life is not the creation of forms**

then

> **the purpose of life is to receive enlightenment and to aid others to become enlightened.**

As one goes deeper and deeper with purpose, one discovers an ideal and purpose that are aligned.

An ideal is what you want to become.
A purpose is a personal benefit.
The greatest personal benefit is to become enlightened.

Therefore, the one with the greatest ideal and the greatest purpose aligns these two.

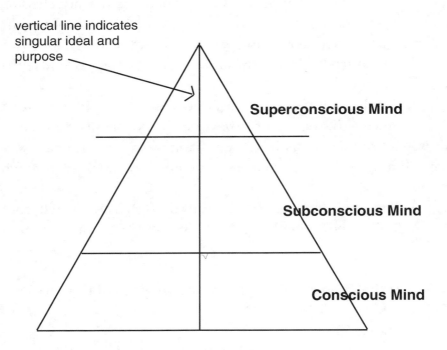

vertical line indicates
singular ideal and
purpose

Superconscious Mind

Subconscious Mind

Conscious Mind

The motivation to discipline the mind comes from a strong desire to know the Self. This strong desire comes from a strong purpose or personal benefit for being enlightened. Enlightenment is the ideal that ignites the conscious mind and consciousness to fan the flame of the desire to know the truth until enlightenment is achieved.

Each person needs the motivation to succeed and the greatest success is enlightenment. It is the work we are here to do.

It is also our duty to help others move forward more rapidly in gaining enlightenment.

People sometimes don't understand the fact that as we learn and progress in Self awareness, we quicken the process by teaching others the knowledge and wisdom we have gained.
Thought to remember:

Permanent understanding of Self is gained through receiving the essence of the life lesson in the experience.
Thought to remember:

Permanent understanding of Self is gained through receiving the essence of the life lesson in the experience.

What to do:

Use your will to place yourself in the experiences to learn.

Use the still mind to then receive the learning in those experiences.

Chapter 14
Enlightenment and Purpose

En-LIGHT-en-ment means to be in the LIGHT of a greater awareness.

When a person has a new idea we say "light bulbs went off in his head" or "there was the dawning of a new awareness in her."

Enlightenment is the continual process of adding to one's awareness and understanding. To be "in the dark" is to be unaware or to not understand.

Why were we put on this green Earth? **We are here to build learning that is permanent and real.**

Basically there are two kinds of learning.

1. There is learning that is temporary.
2. There is learning that is permanent.

The vast majority of people live their lives for the temporary. Many don't focus on learning in life at all.

Each person is here in physical life to learn to know the Self.

Inscribed above the temples of learning of the ancient world was the statement, **"Man, Know Thyself."**

The statement, "Man Know Thyself" is exactly what you are here to do while in a physical life and a physical body.

The word man comes from the Sanskrit word *Manu* and

means thinker. It is not referring to a physical body for a physical body cannot come to know the Self. The word man means thinker, whether in a male or female body.

According to Webster's dictionary, *man* is defined as a human being. While *female* is defined as relating to the sex that performs a fertilizing function.

Man is the human being, a thinker, a soul inhabiting a physical body, that is on planet Earth to learn to become enlightened.

Growing in Self awareness as one's consciousness expands is the result of coming to know the Self. Self growth and Self development give meaning and purpose to life.

How do we learn to become enlightened? By learning what the mind is and how to use it correctly.

Most people exist in the brain. They don't even know what the mind is.

Many people think if they read great books they are exercising their minds. They are not, they are exercising their brains.

Some people think the more facts or information they memorize the more they are using their minds. They are not. What they are doing is storing more information in the brain.

A disciplined mind and imagination is the way to use the mind.
Memory is not the way to use the mind.
A still mind is the way to access consciousness.

How is the mind disciplined? Not in the way most people would expect. The mind is not disciplined by reading more books. Nor is the mind disciplined by trying to think of doing many things at one time. In fact, most of these activities lead to a scattered mind which is the opposite of a disciplined mind.

A person with a disciplined mind is able to focus all of the attention to a single point. Such a one is able and capable of giving full or undivided attention to any person, place or thing at anytime.

Few people have the ability to focus the mind at will anytime.

Fewer still are able to hold the attention focused and concentrated for as long as is desired.

Yet this is exactly what is needed in order to be enlightened.

Before you can know yourself, you must know your thoughts.

Before you can know your thoughts, you must discipline your mind.

In order to discipline your mind, you must first practice concentration and then meditation exercises.

How does concentration discipline the mind? It accomplishes this by giving the mind a singular point of focus. There is a series of continual or repeated choices to hold the attention on the point of focus.

Purpose in life is a point of focus. Some people have such little purpose in life that they have a goal to accumulate physical possessions and a purpose to have more pleasurable sensory experiences. Yet neither of these is permanent and lasting. They come and go. Many of the experiences you have in life you no longer remember. Most people only remember the highlights of some of their most attention getting experiences, be they painful or pleasurable. Yet neither pain nor pleasure determine whether the learning from an experience is integrated into the whole Self where it is stored as permanent memory called understandings.

The really good and productive value of focusing on what

is permanent and lasting is it benefits you forever. Focusing on temporary results or temporary sensory experiences benefits, at best, temporarily and often doesn't even do that. For example, eating lots of sweets may seem to benefit the taste buds' craving yet soon can make one ill if overdone.

The first mental exercise to practice to slow the racing thoughts of the mind is concentration. The thoughts must be slowed down in order that the individual may begin to be aware of the thoughts.

It is only by being aware of the thoughts that one can begin to transcend the thoughts of the conscious mind. Then one can know the thoughts of one's subconscious mind. Following this, one can come to know the thoughts of superconscious mind. Ultimately, one can come to know the thoughts of I AM and LIGHT.

As concentration is practiced regularly and consistently, one will be able to identify any thoughts and say them out loud. The individual develops excellent listening ability and is thus able to hear the thoughts of Self.

At this point one has the capability to allow no limiting thought to go untouched or unnoticed. This gives the person the freedom to adjust, change and adapt the thoughts as needed in order to become a greater, more enlightened being.

The more enlightened one becomes, the more one knows the purpose of life and specifically knows one's own individual purpose.

Some people think it is okay to think negative thoughts in their head, for no one will ever know. It is the person that thinks this way that will never know. For you only come to know the Self as the thoughts are recognized and shared with others.

Learning about oneself through the activity of physical creation is the way we come to know the Self. To ensure this, a still and disciplined mind is required. A mind that has an ideal to become is required. A mind with a purpose is required and needed.

The Universal LIGHT is made up of Universal Truth and Universal Love.

Universal LIGHT manifests as Universal Truth and Universal Love in the Universal Subconscious Mind and in our physical universe.

In Superconscious Mind, LIGHT manifests as the Aggressive and Receptive Principles of Creation — Mind.

Exercise to practice
Practice saying all your thoughts out loud for a day.
Notice what your thoughts sound like. Listen to the words that are the verbalization of your thoughts. Be diligent with it and use it throughout the day. Judge your thoughts. Are they productive or unproductive? Are they positive or are they negative? Are they blame thoughts or do you accept that you create your life?

Be diligent. When you notice a limiting thought or a limitation in consciousness, replace it with a better thought or attitude, one that is in alignment with Love, Truth and LIGHT. Accept the fact that you create your life the way it is and therefore you can cause it to be different.

Thought to Remember
The essence of your being is LIGHT, spiritually, mentally, emotionally and physically. Grow in awareness and grow in LIGHT.

What to do:
Practice concentration and meditation to know purpose.

Chapter 15
The Superconscious, Subconscious and Conscious Mind and Purpose

Consider yourself as a multi-dimensional being. Consider that you exist on more than one level of Mind at once. In other words, you are not only a physical body and a brain. You are also a conscious mind being, a subconscious mind being and a superconscious mind being.

What is the conscious mind? The conscious mind is that part of yourself that works in conjunction with the physical body, which includes the physical brain.

When a person functions from habit then that person is allowing the brain to control the Self. Brain pathways are habits. Habits are brain pathways.

When a person exercises the will by making choices then that person is using the conscious mind.

Most people think they have or are using free will and imagination when in fact they are thinking 90 to 95 percent of the same thoughts every day.

Why do people repeat the same thoughts day after day? It is because those thoughts are already stored as mental images in the brain. These memories impinge on the present moment colorizing and distorting perceptions of the present moment. It is as if a filter has been placed on one's perceptions. And that filter renders the person incapable of perceiving the present moment accurately.

On the other hand, some people view each day as a new creation. They have created goals and are determined to succeed and go beyond their own limitations be they mental, emotional or physical.

Some people visualize their ideal Self. They may have an ideal of being like Christ or being a Christ or a Buddha. In other words, such individuals have an ideal of being enlightened. They attempt to live this ideal every day and thereby reach and stretch to go beyond all limitations. Such people discipline their minds in order to more effectively exercise their will and imaging capabilities.

As the conscious mind is disciplined it becomes more and more aligned with one's subconscious mind.

The subconscious mind is the abode of your soul. More accurately, subconscious mind is the abode of you as a soul. For you see, you are a soul inhabiting a physical body. The soul is eternal. The physical body, brain and conscious mind are temporary. The subconscious mind is permanent and lasting. Which are you going to live your life for?

If you choose to live your life for what is permanent and lasting then it is imperative to discipline the mind and discover your purpose in life. Your purpose is never physical yet may manifest itself or show itself in physical ways.

Your purpose may be to understand love or truth or value or communication or caring or giving or importance. These purposes are not physical things yet they can be in your life in everything you do and every interaction. These qualities or understandings can be in your consciousness throughout the day. They can affect everything you think, do and say. They affect your attitudes and your consciousness.

It is the qualities of being and understanding that enhance our lives and our consciousness. It is a truth that "as we think so we become."

Therefore, in order for one to grow in awareness and fulfill the soul's purpose in this lifetime, one must think greater, more truth-filled and elevated thoughts.

As one imagines and lives higher and higher ideals, one enters into the realm of superconscious mind. This is the abode of spirit which is sometimes called the Real Self.

One who achieves the superconscious state lives the life of supreme fulfillment. Such a one lives the life to fulfill not only his or her purpose but also to fulfill the greater purpose of uplifting the consciousness of the entire planet and everyone on it.

As one realizes these higher and higher states of mind, consciousness and purpose, the fulfillment in life grows and expands until one comes to know all of creation and all beings as connected.

Then one fulfills the highest purpose as a world teacher or a world savior, an enlightened being that comes to enlighten the world.

In order to fulfill one's purpose in connection with subconscious mind there must be the willingness to learn about oneself in every experience. There must be the willingness and effort to receive into the Self the essence of the learning in each and every experience.

If you really want to discover and fulfill your purpose you are going to have to change. Sooner or later everyone changes anyway. It is just a question of whether you will cause the changes and growth in wisdom within yourself or will you be dragged kicking and screaming by life's circumstances as the world around you changes?

The nature of the physical is change. Everything around us changes. Sometimes things around us appear to be permanent yet if you will search your memory you will find that there are a lot of things that have physically changed since you were a child, including your physical body. Your physical body continues to change. What will you choose to do with the precious days, weeks, months and year that you have here on Mother Earth?

How much can you discover and understand about your life's purpose in a day, a week, a month or a year? How much can you come to understand about the purpose of life in that amount of time?

By choosing to discipline the mind through concentration and meditation, one can become more proficient and efficient in drawing forth the learning in every experience.

Everyone needs a teacher in order to learn the keys for knowing mind and Self. If you don't know where to start in discovering your purpose or you don't know how to meditate, it may be time for you to find a teacher: someone who knows how to teach the mind, someone who knows how to teach the student how to discipline the mind in order to know the Self. If this is what you are interested in you can find resources at the back of this book.

I have been a student all my life. I have also been a teacher most of my adult life.

Once you discover more about your purpose and the purpose of life you may want to share this knowledge with others.

The world needs more teachers, and the world needs more people that are students, people that are always willing to learn whether they are age 7 or 70.

You can come to know your Real Self, your High Self, yourself as a soul, and you can fulfill your purpose.

Once the conscious and subconscious minds are aligned you may then attune them to superconscious mind.

In subconscious mind you will experience a more connected consciousness. You will experience a feeling and knowing how everything you think, do and say affects everyone else.

In superconscious mind you will experience a oneness in consciousness. You will experience a oneness with all creation and everyone and everything in it.

It is good and wonderful to know your purpose in life and very few people do. Yet even to know your purpose in life is not the end. Learning your purpose in life is, in many ways, a beginning. For as your purpose is learned and practiced, it continues to unfold. As your purpose unfolds, it continues to amaze you with the insights, awareness and understanding you gain of yourself, life, people and all creation.

There is no end to learning and there is no end to the enlightened being you can become. Each of us are born to fulfill a great mission. Some do, some don't.

The mission isn't to become famous, although some highly evolved souls do. The mission is to come to know the Self, to fill one's subconscious mind or soul with permanent understandings of Self and Creation and to become enlightened.

By disciplining the conscious mind and through aiding others to do the same, one offers the highest service. For thought is cause and only by coming to know one's own thoughts will one come to know Self, God and Creation.

It is through service to others that we open our hearts to aid others to live a higher life and thereby more fully enable ourselves to experience a higher life, a higher consciousness called superconscious awareness and cosmic consciousness.

Thought to remember:
     The mind is the vehicle to know the Self.

What to do:
     Discipline the mind.
     A disciplined mind can transform your life.

Chapter 16
Overcoming Limitations
to Fulfill Your Purpose
Making a Choice

Often people are unaware of the ways in which they limit or restrict themselves. People tend to be unconscious of the very thoughts and attitudes that hold them back and keep them from achieving their greatest desires.

In order to fulfill your purpose you must become aware of the thoughts and attitudes that are unconscious. If a thought is unconscious then you did not choose the thought. If you did not choose the thought then who or what did choose the thought? If you did not choose the thought then your brain is re-acting out of old memory images. The brain stores memory images. The environment will stimulate these old memory images. When this occurs the stimulated memory images in the brain appear as thoughts. These memories have been accessed.

Sometimes these memory images may be totally inappropriate for the present situation. This is the source of most reactions. Sometimes these memory images can help solve a problem in the present. The difficulty arises when we are not consciously choosing to draw forth memories or any other thought.

To fulfill the life purpose one must wake up to a higher consciousness and to higher awareness in one's thoughts and being. That higher purpose is available to one who has a higher awareness.

How does one gain this higher awareness? By being aware of one's thoughts. How does one gain awareness of one's thoughts? By practicing mental discipline.

Mental discipline, such as concentration exercises, enables one to slow down the thoughts and to cease the idle chatter going on in the conscious mind and brain.

When the thoughts in the mind move at a rapid rate, trying to know the thoughts is like trying to know a movie in fast motion. You may get a few details or the general idea, but for the most part you really don't experience the movie.

Slow the thoughts down until you can cause the thoughts to stop. Then the mind can be still. In order to still the mind you must make a choice. The choice is to stop thinking. By this I do not mean to stop thinking forever. Rather the perspective shifts from thinking incessantly to the perspective of a still mind that then chooses a thought.

To function from a still mind is to find and achieve the ability to choose and the ability to create.

(Choosing and creating are essential to understanding your purpose in life.)

In order to still the mind you must first make a choice. The choice must be to focus the mind on one point or place. By focusing on one point there is, at that time, no need for thought. When there is no need for thought, the mind can be still. (The mind is still in the space between thoughts.)

In that stillness you will come to know your purpose. In the stillness the outer conscious mind is aligned with the inner subconscious mind.

One's individual purpose for a lifetime comes from one's subconscious mind.

As the still and quiet mind continues to be practiced the individual experiences an attunement of conscious and subconscious minds to superconscious mind. Then one realizes the higher purpose of service to all of mankind, all of humanity.

The fulfillment of this superconscious purpose is actually the culmination of the ideal of enlightenment. It is the world teacher, the enlightened master. It is the Buddha consciousness, the Christ consciousness and the cosmic consciousness. This achievement requires a mastery of the mind and the ability to choose either a still mind or a mind in motion, at will, anytime.

Thought to remember:
Consistently think greater thoughts and you become greater.
Consistently think more productive thoughts and become more productive.

What to do:
Improve your thoughts each day.

Chapter 17
Service and Purpose

Sooner or later each person comes to realize that in order to completely fulfill the purpose in life one must offer service to others. Yes, you must be committed to your learning and growth. You must also be willing to aid other people to improve and lead better or greater lives.

The truth is, we are all intimately connected. The true nature of reality is connectedness. Our five senses of sight, smell, taste, touch and hearing seem to say one person is separate from another person.

If you are across the room from a person or half a world away it may seem as if you are separate. Yet, remember a time when you were in love or loved someone very deeply. At those times you were very, very connected to each other.

All is connected in LIGHT, love and Universal Truth.

It is because of this connection that each person must come to realize the need for aiding others to prosperity and abundance. Abundance can mean accumulation of money or wealth. Abundance can also be emotional and mental. Prosperity is the ability to produce repeated success. Prosperity is the ability to continually improve and add to any situation or circumstance one places the Self in.

Most, and probably all, success any person has in life is due to the help or aid of one or more other people. Think about it. Someone had to give you food, shelter and clothing in order for you to grow to adulthood. Someone gave you your first job.

Someone taught you in school or elsewhere. All these benefits we receive and more. And from this giving we grew. Therefore, as adults, it is important for us to remember to give back what we have received and more.

For it is in giving that we receive.

For it is in giving that we learn.

For it is in giving that we gain a greater ability to receive.

For it is in giving that we become more connected to those to whom we give.

For it is in giving that we grow in love.

For it is in giving that we become more capable of receiving love.

For it is in giving that we become more capable of learning and understanding the universal truth.

For it is in giving that we gain more friends.

For it is giving to those greater than us that we become greater.

For it is in giving to those who know more that we come to know more.

For it is in giving to one's teacher that one learns how to teach.

For it is in giving and receiving that one learns to be connected.

For it is in giving that one comes to forgive.

For it is in giving gratitude that one learns to forgive.

For it is in giving that we come to receive the true nature of reality.

Development of the still mind and knowing your purpose in life takes time and effort. The good news is you can make progress every day once you know what you are doing.

In order to learn and grow you need a humble, teachable attitude. You have to be willing to accept and cause growthful change.

Repetition enables one to develop a skill. Concentration and meditation are skills.

Service

The hallmark of adulthood in reasoning is to produce more than you consume. You are on this Earth to add to what is already here. When you help and serve others you are serving God and aiding humanity to improve and develop.

It is often our natural inclination to want to help ourselves first. Yet Jesus said, "Do unto others as you would have them do unto you."

This demonstrates a scientific principal that, "As you sow, so shall you reap." As you give so will you receive.

Therefore, giving is of personal benefit to the giver because the giver receives more than the hoarder or the miser.

Your heart relates to your motivation. Your heart relates to what you love to do.

Most exceptionally talented and gifted children as well as Indigo children have abilities and desires that the rest of the family isn't even interested in or cares about.

When you have purpose for things you do, you develop greater heart, passion and compassion. You develop an enthusiasm or greater joy for living.

Look at your abilities and talents. How are you using these to aid others in their growth and Self awareness?

In order to truly know your purpose you must discipline your mind. In this way the mind becomes the vehicle, the tool, for you, the individual, to use.

Meditation and concentration do not give enlightenment. Meditation and concentration give you the opportunity to use the experiences of life correctly to gain enlightenment.

The more permanent understandings of Self that you have built prior to incarning into this life the more likely you are to manifest a lot of abilities, talents or "so called" gifts.

As you give service to others, you will more and more discover your talents, abilities and understandings.

Use mental discipline to still the mind and receive the essence of the learning from all experiences.

Always be willing to try new thing like teaching and lecturing so that you may bring out these hidden talents, gifts and understandings. Do your duty, not the duty of another, so you can fulfill what you are here to do.

All great spiritual teachers from Jesus the Christ to Guatama the Buddha, from Appolonius of Tyana to Pythagoras have given service. Service, when practiced with purpose, elevates our consciousness and helps fulfill our purpose on Earth.

To be like these great Spiritual masters is to be a servant, which is to serve. Real service is doing what is needed even when it is uncomfortable.

Soul growth and spiritual development is a process of stretching and reaching. Comfort never quickened one's enlightenment.

What you do does not have to be perfect. Most things in physical life are not perfect. If you wait until things are perfect to respond you may wait forever. To wait forever is to be passive and to procrastinate. One who gives service consistently with joy develops an open heart and is full of love.

Purpose provides the motivation to give service.

One can give service upward to those with greater authority and understanding or downward to those that want to learn what you know.

Those that give service think often about others. This helps to develop humility in oneself.

There are three great questions of life.

1. Who am I?
2. What am I here to do?
3. What am I here to become?

Everyone has weaknesses and failures. Therefore, do not use this as an excuse for getting started at service.

Admit your weaknesses. Then go about building them into strengths.

Remember to always share. Satan, which is the conscious ego, doesn't want you to share because the ego sees this as a loss.

The high truth is that sharing and giving produce a great gain for the Self, the soul.

By sharing you can grow with others. People don't become enlightened by themselves. We become enlightened in connectedness with others.

Mature, adult reasoners develop the ability to receive the life lessons from every experience and apply them universally.

To find your purpose in life, meditate and listen.

In order to <u>serve</u> your purpose in life:

1. Identify what you know to be true based upon what you have made a part of yourself.
2. Place yourself in a position of service, teaching others what you have learned.

Thought to remember:
>The one who serves is served.
>The one who gives, receives.

Exercise to practice:
>Practice giving service of some kind every day, no matter how small or how large.

Chapter 18
Love , Open Mind, Open Heart, and Purpose

What are some keys to having an open mind and an open heart?

1. **Gratitude**
2. **Thankfulness**
3. **Forgiveness**
4. **Enjoying learning**
5. **Security**
6. **Openness to each experience**
7. **Love**
8. **Being determined to know the truth**
9. **Living the truth**
10. **Appreciation**
11. **Self Value**
12. **Mental Discipline**
13. **Receptivity**

All of the above cause the Self to have an openness to learning. An openness to learning provides an opportunity to be open to receive the learning of one's purpose from the soul or subconscious mind of Self.

Love people with an open heart. It is difficult to love when one is closed off to the world.

Love enables one to be open to receive the learning in every experience.

In order to learn of one's purpose, the mind must be open.

In order to know one's purpose, the heart must be open also.

How are these two, an open heart and an open mind, created? They are created from the discipline of the mind and the desire to know.

What is it that one needs to know? One needs to know the Self and all Creation.

Love opens the heart.

Truth opens the mind.

Where the heart and mind are open then can the Real Self be known.

Love makes the lessons of life easier to receive.

Purpose enables one to recognize or create a benefit in each experience.

Therefore, love and purpose go hand in hand. As you benefit, others can also benefit. As you share the learning with love and an open heart, the benefits of each experience accrue to you and others.

To live in an environment without love usually indicates a situation where people are not very open to receiving from one another. Often they are also closed off to giving.

Because the true nature of reality is connectedness, love enables one to align with this true reality. Love opens one up to give freely and to receive freely. In giving and receiving freely, one is more closely connected with others and the world around the Self.

Gratitude helps one have an open mind and an open heart by causing the Self to be in the present.

When one can experience gratitude for the experiences of the past then the attention is brought more fully into the present. This is because when benefits of an experience are recognized, they override hurts from that experience.

By being more fully in the present, one can experience greater love and greater purpose. Both love and purpose are present time. Purpose, which is personal benefit, is in the present.

Gratitude and gratefulness is given for what one has already received. To receive a personal benefit is to fulfill a purpose.

A series of directed purposes leads to the fulfillment of one's life purpose.

Thankfulness and forgiveness also work hand in hand with love and purpose. Both thankfulness and forgiveness bring one into the present.

Remember gratitude enables one to see how Self benefits in each experience.

Forgiveness enables one to give, for the purpose of receiving more. To forgive is to give for a purpose and that purpose is the upliftment of one's consciousness.

Thankfulness strengthens the results gained from forgiveness by emphasizing the benefits one has gained.

Love makes everything easier. Love makes the learning easy to receive. Thankfulness and gratitude bring one into the present where one can receive. Purpose is always in the present.

Purpose aids one to know Self as "I AM," which is also present time. To know Self as I AM, which is one's true individuality, one must be in present time.

Consider when you have felt safe and secure. Usually it is when there is love associated with the experience.

When feeling safe and secure, it is easier to receive the learning in each situation. It is <u>easier</u> to be connected, and connectedness is the true nature of reality.

A person living in a state of fear will find it difficult to allow the LIGHT of awareness to enter into the Self.

Love not only creates an openness to receive, it also has a warmth and drawing power to it.

People are drawn to warmth. People are drawn to love.

An open mind enables one to receive truth.

An open heart enables one to receive love.

Together love and truth enable one to be filled with LIGHT.

Since many people lack either an open mind or an open heart, they must also lack purpose.

What causes a person to be closed off to life and learning?

        1. Fear

        2. Anger

        3. Hatred

        4. Doubt

        5. Insecurity

        6. Guilt

        7. Condemnation

        8. Greed

        9. Sensory engrossment

        10. Self pity

        11. Manipulation

        12. Low self worth

        13. Undisciplined mind

Being closed off is usually based upon fear. Fear is a learned re-action to life. Fear can be overcome by love. Love opens the Self to receive the LIGHT of awareness. Fear is of the unknown and of the darkness, of lack of awareness.

Love often reaches people when nothing else can. Love connects people. Love connects people in the heart.

When people have stopped loving because of fear they need a purpose. This purpose is a personal benefit for opening once again.

In order to learn the universal lessons of life you have to become open to receive those lessons.

If you will observe every time you get hurt intentionally or unintentionally by another, the natural or normal re-action is to close off for protection. The difficulty arises when the protective wall remains even after the event has passed. Then the individual needs a motivating purpose in order to come out of the prison of Self created limitations.

Love for others brings one out of the darkness of fear. Purpose provides the incentive to move, to change and to grow. By loving others one grows in awareness and Self value.

Any of these 13 qualities can cause you to become closed off to learning and fulfilling your purpose in life.

Hatred and anger cause a person to push other people away. It also causes one to push the lessons of life away.

Fear causes one to close off to the lessons of life.

Doubt and insecurity keeps one from acting and responding to life.

Condemnation keeps one in the past, and therefore, incapable of responding in the present.

Greed keeps a person engrossed in attaining physical possessions. The purpose of life is not physical. The purpose of life embodies those qualities that make for an enlightened soul.

Sensory engrossment keeps one's attention bound up in physical substance. In this way also a person will miss the purpose of life.

Self pity keeps one from acting on goals and ideals in the present in much the same way as doubt.

Manipulation is a way to physically attempt to control a situation instead of mentally directing one's mind. Thus, it will keep one physically bound while missing the purpose of life.

Low self worth keeps one from taking the initiative in acting on desires, needs, goals and ideals. The solution to low self worth is in giving and receiving freely every day.

An undisciplined mind will keep one from achieving the purpose of life. A disciplined mind is necessary to know one's own thoughts. A disciplined mind is necessary to know the Self. A disciplined mind is needed to still the restless thoughts of the mind in order that one may receive one's purpose from the inner Self.

A way to practice each day, throughout the day, to discern, live and fulfill one's purpose is to ask yourself in each experience, "is this temporary or permanent?" In other words is the experience I am having now permanent and lasting? Strive to discover the lesson in each experience.

The true lesson of life in each experience will always be lasting and permanent.

For example, suppose the lesson in an experience concerns love. Once gained, the lessons of life incorporated into Self are permanent and everlasting.

The lesson may be about value, pride, humbleness, authority, dignity, commitment, or any number of other qualities that improve one's character and being.

The important thing to keep in mind is that each person should strive to learn the lessons of life that make one a better, more loving, more enlightened being.

Universal love, universal truth, and universal LIGHT are the Universal, overall lessons to be gained or learned in any and all experience.

Thought to remember:

An open mind and an open heart enable one to receive life's purpose.

Love makes everything work better.

Exercise to practice:

Visualize your heart opening to life. Strive to add love to each experience.

Chapter 19
Concentration, Meditation and Purpose

The best exercise to practice to begin mental discipline is concentration. This is because the practice of concentration enables one to not only focus and direct the mind more effectively, it also enables one to be more aware of one's thoughts.

How can you know your purpose if you don't know your own thoughts. Even though most of the thoughts people think each day are repetitive thoughts, they nonetheless are unconscious or unaware of many or most of those thoughts. This means that even though most thoughts are repetitive, people are not consciously choosing those thoughts. It is as if people are on automatic pilot or asleep or half asleep.

Will can only be exercised when choices are made. How many conscious choices do you make each day? Do you eat just because you are hungry? Do you eat from habit? Do you eat when you are not hungry? Do you eat just because it is time to eat? Do you choose to eat each bit of food or do you just eat as fast as you can gulp it down because it tastes good?

This is one example of how most people are not conscious or awake and instead function from habit or an undisciplined mind.

It is not an easy thing to do, but the mind can be mastered. It requires will and discipline. Concentration is the key. In order to concentrate one needs to choose where to place one's attention. Suppose you want to concentrate on the tip of your finger. At first you will place your attention on the tip of your finger. If your attention wanders someplace else you will bring it back. Suppose your attention drifts to a talk you had with a friend yesterday. If this occurs you will bring your attention back to the tip of your finger. Suppose your attention wanders to an itch on your face, then you will need to bring your attention back to the tip of your finger.

When practicing concentration, it is best to practice on a still or non-moving object. If the object moves too much it ends up being a stimulation experience instead of a concentration exercise.

Some people like to drive cars or trucks a lot. When the car or truck is moving down the highway the mind is entertained by the panorama of scenery. This is not concentration. Being entertained as the scenery constantly changes causes the mind to move. Concentration causes the mind to become more focused, still and alive.

A concentrated, focused mind is more efficient, effective, and productive than a busy or scattered mind.

The busy, scattered mind is diffused thereby losing its power and effectiveness.

A concentrated, focused, still mind has all of its attention directed to a single place or point thus causing powerful results

Why is concentration necessary for purpose? Why is concentration necessary to know one's purpose? Because without concentration one drifts into old habits and old brain pathways stored in the brain. The brain is a physical organ of the physical body. Whereas one's life purpose comes from one's subconscious mind.

The physical brain can never give you your purpose in life. To know one's purpose one must use the part or division of mind that works directly with the brain, known as the conscious mind.

The conscious mind, when disciplined can be caused to open to receive the insights, awarenesses and understandings of subconscious mind. For it is your inner subconscious mind that chose your purpose for this lifetime before you were born.

It is the duty and responsibility of the conscious mind to use the brain and the rest of the physical body wisely to discover and fulfill one's life purpose while here on this physical Earth.

Purpose is personal benefit, and the highest benefit is fulfilling one's purpose to cause a quickening of one's soul awareness and to aid others to the same.

When the mind is stilled, one can receive direction, perception and insight from subconscious mind. This wisdom and higher knowledge does not and cannot originate from the brain.

The brain is good at physical things such as calculations and solving problems. The brain is pretty good at storing memories. The physical body is an animal body, albeit a highly evolved one. Does this mean that we are animals? No, for unlike animals, people have a mind. Each individual can either choose to learn to develop and use their mind or they can choose to remain entrapped in the physical brain with all its attendant limitations.

The choice to live in the physical brain is the choice to identify with the animal body. When this choice is made the person may lead a very habitual, animalistic life or the person may be very smart and cunning. The person will not, however, become enlightened this way and will at best fulfill only a small portion of her purpose.

In order to listen effectively one must stop thinking. The person who is constantly thinking while another person is talking will, at best, only receive a small portion of what the other person is saying.

The individual who is genuinely interested in what the other person has to say will have his or her attention focused or riveted on the person who is speaking. Such a one desires to receive what the other person has to say. Such a one has stilled and directed the mind to be able to receive more than what was previously available.

Do your thoughts control you or do you control your thoughts? To determine this, choose to place your attention on one point or thing. Notice how quickly your attention moves to something else, seemingly involuntarily? When your attention moves somewhere other than the place or thing you have chosen, this indicates the mind or the brain is controlling you rather than you, the individual, directing the mind and the brain.

Have you ever learned a skill? Everyone has learned some skills. Even walking and talking are skills. If you will remember the skills you developed as an adult, you will notice that they required attention, effort and practice while you were developing them. The development of purpose in the life also requires consistent and regular practice, attention and effort.

Therefore, the question, "What is my purpose for my activity in the present moment?" will get you thinking along the lines of a personal benefit for every thing you do.

Life is meant to be a personal benefit. Life is designed or meant to be of permanent or lasting benefit to the whole Self.

Eating your favorite food is a temporary satisfaction. Seeing a movie or theatre play you enjoy is a temporary thrill. So what gives lasting fulfillment? Lasting fulfillment occurs when the conscious and subconscious minds are aligned through mental discipline and concentration. The still conscious mind is open and receptive thus aligning itself with the understanding, wisdom and high knowledge the subconscious mind has to offer.

Using only the conscious mind and not the subconscious mind is like having one hand tied behind your back.

Using only the brain without consciously using the subconscious and conscious minds is like having both hands tied behind your back.

Without the power, wisdom and insight that comes from a disciplined mind, the individual moves through life severely handicapped and ineffectual concerning the true meaning of life and how to fulfill it. This is because the meaning of life is not physical and will not be found in temporary, sensory stimulation experiences.

The purpose of life can only be discovered and fulfilled when the individual learns to draw the permanent and lasting learning from the experiences. To do this requires a disciplined mind, a receptive mind, and a focused mind.

To learn to draw the essence of the learning from every experience requires knowledge and training in the Universal Laws and Universal Truth that form the framework and structure of all of mind and all of creation.

In coming to know our purpose in life it is necessary that more and more we come to know Self. This is necessary because one's purpose revolves around and involves Self. Even helping others involves oneself.

In order to come to know the Self, one must have a disciplined mind. For mind is the tool, the vehicle, for knowing Self.

The most powerful tool for knowing the Self is concentration for concentration focuses and disciplines the mind of the individual practicing it.

The second most powerful tool for knowing the Self is meditation. Meditation may be considered the most powerful tool, yet if one does not know how to concentrate then one's meditation may be ineffectual.

Concentration gives one or more of the senses a point to focus upon while meditation closes off the senses to physical, sensory experiences. Because people have practiced all their lives giving attention to sensory experiences, it works best to use one or more of the senses to begin building the power of the mind.

In order to know the power of the mind there must be discipline. Discipline gives control. To use the vehicle of the mind properly there must be the ability to direct one's mind.

Think about this. If your mind is silent, who are you?

Just who are you without any thoughts? People who have great enlightenment and discovered their purpose in life have learned to identify their thoughts. Then they separate out the productive from unproductive thoughts. Over time they think fewer and fewer thoughts. Then the mind can be used by the thinker as a tool to create.

Creation always begins as a state of stillness. Next the stillness transforms to a state of expectant non-action called receptivity.

A quality that is developed as one gains greater mastery of the mind is receptivity. The quality of receptivity becomes more and more obvious, more and more prevalent, in the individual who practices mental discipline. Far from being passive, such a one is a dynamic center of love, LIGHT, truth and wisdom.

To gain receptivity is to enhance one's ability to receive. The greater one's capacity to receive, the greater one's ability to draw the learning into the Self that is needed in any situation. This greater capacity includes the ability to discern the the learning for the whole Self that is lasting and eternal.

If you are angry, you don't have a still mind.
If you are mad, you don't have a still mind.
If you are vengeful, you don't have a still mind.
If you are guilty, you don't have a still mind.
If you are indignant, you don't have a still mind.

A still mind is the basis for all real power.

Low Self worth does not exist in a still mind.

Low Self respect does not exist in a still mind.
Low Self esteem does not exist in a still mind.
Low Self value does not exist in a still mind.

Understanding one's value begins by having productive thoughts that come forth from a still mind.

Improving one's ability to focus and direct the mind takes nothing away from what one had before. Discipline of the mind gives one choice, the freedom to choose.

In order to achieve one's purpose in life the strengthening of one's will and the building of will power is imperative.

Building the will does not mean just doing more activity. Will power is a series of unceasing and committed efforts toward a physical goal or a mental ideal.

Will power is the continuous choice to go or move towards the goal or ideal that has been created.

People often fail to achieve their purpose in life because they fail to have enough value in themselves to believe they can have what is imaged or desired.

Value can only be gained in the present moment, and the present moment is the only time and place you can fully give your attention.

Thought to remember:
	The present is better than the past.
	The present is better than the future.

Exercise to practice:
	Say to yourself each day: I exist in the present moment.

Chapter 20
The <u>Bible</u> , Christianity and Purpose

In this chapter I will cover some ideas about purpose from what might be described as a mainline Christian perspective as well as the perspective of consciousness.

1. You discover your identity and purpose through a relationship with Jesus Christ.

Now let us consider what a relationship with Jesus Christ means or entails.

Christ is a word borrowed from the Greek language.

Christos or *Christ* means anointed. It is equivalent in meaning to the word enlightened and also the word messiah.

There were several anointed Greeks or Greek Christs. That is why the Greeks had a word for anointed.

To have a relationship with Christ is to build a connection with your own Christ consciousness. What is Christ consciousness? Christ consciousness is the development of the enlightened Self. It is the receiving of superconscious mind into the Self.

The name Jesus is also a Greek version of the name Joshua. In other words Jesus' real name is Joshua. Joshua was a mighty General of the Israelites in the Old Testament. Joshua led the Israelites into the promised land and overcame all obstacles because he did what the Lord (I AM) commanded.

Jesus became enlightened and thus became a Messiah, a Christ. That is, he became a savior for mankind. What did Jesus the Christ save people from? He saved people from their sins. What are sins? Sins are mistakes. What kind of mistakes? Mistakes are any experience that fails to add permanent learning of Self and Creation to the soul. Mistakes are any distractions that lead one away from the true purpose of life.

Your High Self is the Christ within. You can develop expanded consciousness and cosmic consciousness. This is why it is possible to develop a relationship with Jesus who became the Christ. Jesus the Christ developed cosmic consciousness. Therefore, he can be and is everywhere because his consciousness is expanded to fill all of Mind.

Of course there is a Creator of all creation. And of course the Creator has a plan for us that is Universal and general.

Specifically within that framework of learning to be creators, we choose our purpose each lifetime. This we do in order to learn the lessons needed to become a creator.

2. God created your purpose.

Yes, God created you and has a purpose for you. That purpose is to be like the Creator, as given in Genesis 1:26, "Then God said, 'Let us make man in our image, after our likeness.'"

So we are descended from the plural God as given by the words *us* and *our*. *Us* and *our* indicate both the aggressive and receptive qualities contained in the Creator. So it is our responsibility to understand the aggressive and receptive qualities in ourselves.

The statement to be made after our likeness, means to be created with like or similar attributes. What are the attributes of a creator? One of those attributes is to be able to image or imagine or visualize what you desire to create and then to cause that visualized image to become a part of your outward life.

So you have a purpose or personal benefit of learning to be a creator by utilizing your imaging capabilities.

Within that scope of experience you, as a soul, choose each lifetime's experience for the purpose of learning some aspect of creation. That aspect may be love, wisdom, truth, receptivity, insight, caring, kindness, nurturing, communication or any host of other qualities.

Therefore, each lifetime each person has an individual purpose to fulfill that fits into the overall scheme or purpose of becoming enlightened like our Creator.

You chose the basic qualities or factors of your life before you were born, and incarned.

You chose to be male or female. You chose what country you were born into. You chose your race. You even chose when you would be born, even if you don't remember this. The talents you came into this life with you developed and brought with you.

No one is an accident. This is why it is so vitally important for each of us to use our talents, skills and understandings to help others. This is why it is so important for parents to understand that children are not just little physical bodies. Children are big souls with much wisdom encased in a child's or baby's body.

Yes, God created us. And he also gave us free will so we could learn to be like him. Otherwise, there would be no purpose to creation and to ourselves. We would just be senseless automatons.

You are not an accident because you chose your life and you create your life.

Even though we are products of the past we do not have to let the past control us. Each moment is a choice. Yet most people refuse to make that choice.

If you hold on to resentment, guilt or anger then you live in the past. There is no purpose in the past. Purpose can only flourish and exist in the present.

Therefore, as often as possible keep your attention in the present. Strive to move more and more of your attention to the present.

The present is where fulfillment exists.

Fear also keeps you locked in the prison of the past. Replace fear with desire. Purpose creates desire. Replace fear with the light of awareness. Fear is of the darkness. Dispel fear by shining the Light of attention and understanding on it.

Educate yourself concerning your fear. Do not avoid fear. Fear will not go away by avoiding fear. Instead separate and identify your thoughts.

Trying to please everyone is a sure key to failure because you can't please everyone. Plus, pleasing everyone is not your purpose.

Each person needs to learn to create purpose for the life. Yet an undisciplined mind has difficulty creating purpose.

An undisciplined mind is too scattered and too much in the past to create purpose.

To have effective purpose, the mind must be focused enough to create goals, ideals and directed activity.

Without purpose, life has little meaning. There may be motion and movement in the life and activity without direction. Yet the Self fails to learn the real lessons of life, the Universal Laws and Universal Truths.

Discovering and fulfilling your purpose simplifies your life.

Your purpose focuses your mind to what you want to receive and what you want to do. Purpose thereby helps to eliminate distractions.

Ask yourself, "Does this activity help me fulfill my purpose in life?"

The more you practice purpose every day, the more you discover purpose in your life. The more you discover purpose, the greater your ability to make productive decisions and thus build your spiritual foundation.

It is impossible to do everything every person may want you to do. You have just enough time to fulfill your purpose and assignment for this lifetime. Therefore, use every moment productively.

Living a purpose fulfilled life leads to a simpler life because the deeper levels of mind are simple and uncomplicated.

Knowing your purpose for this lifetime focuses your energies in this lifetime on what is important.

Most people go round and round but never get to the meaning of life. Without a clear purpose you keep changing things in your outer life and in your environment hoping that physical change will fill the emptiness you are feeling and experiencing in your life.

Many people are busy without a purpose because they have busy minds. Activity does not always produce learning and self awareness. Motion does not always produce learning.

Purpose always produces motivation and passion.

Jesus the Christ said, "I must be about my Father's business." Luke 2:49.

Your Father's business is your business. Your business is fulfilling your life's purpose.

Recognize your purpose is a mighty one.

Knowing your purpose prepares you for eternity, the eternal now, by aiding you to build permanent understandings of Self and Creation. You are here on Earth to build permanent understandings of Self and Creation. This is your eternal, permanent and lasting legacy! This is wisdom.

Are you living your life for yourself or are you living your life for others or both?

The physical life is not all there is to life, being and existence. Yet this life in a physical body is very valuable to draw the permanent and eternal learning into the Self.

Your physical, earthly body is just a temporary residence for you the soul, the Real Self.

When you fully understand that there is more to life than just the past and future in physical existence then you will live more and more in the eternal, present now. When you live in the present you begin to live differently because you really experience life.

The eternal present is everything. This why Jesus said, "Before Abraham was I AM." *John 8:58.*

I AM is present tense. Otherwise Jesus would have said, "before Abraham was, I was." Which refers to the past. If referring to the future, Jesus would have said, "Before Abraham was, I will be."

Jesus was referring to the ever present, eternal now.

When you live in the Light of the ever present, eternal now, your perspective changes. You use your attention, energy and time more wisely.

You tend to view life through the filter of your own attitude, memories and habits.

Life is a test in that you are here to learn the essence of life that physical experiences offer. Most people do not know how to receive or draw the essence of the learning in each experience. In order to pass the test of life you need to learn how to learn.

There is far more to life than just the few years we live on this planet. I AM, the real you, exists always and forever and is beyond time.

Don't get attached to what is around you because it is temporary. Cultivate the still mind. The conscious mind is always trying to figure solutions to problems. The still mind receives all answers and all solutions.

Christians say you must be born again to become truly saved from your sins. Yet, what does being born again mean? "Except ye be born again, ye shall not see the Kingdom of God." *John 3:3.* The deep inner secret to being born again into each level of consciousness is to gain subconscious and superconscious awareness and understanding. You can be born into a higher dimension of reality.

This is a great secret to entering the Kingdom of God called heaven. Do everything with a still mind and receive the full experience. Then make a choice to move, to create and to be.

The Superconscious Mind is Heaven.

When a man first falls in love with a woman he thinks about her constantly.

When a woman first falls in love with a man she thinks about him constantly. However, to know God, do not think at all.

Real worship of God is to gain the Still Mind. For as the <u>Bible</u> says, "Be still and know that I AM is a god." *Psalms 46:10.*

To know the Creator is to know yourself as a son or daughter of the Creator. To know the Creator is to know Self as I AM.

We must come to love the growth of the soul. We must learn to love soul growth and spiritual development. Let your greatest purpose be to add to your consciousness every day and to align with the Universal Laws and Universal Truths.

It is important to practice obedience and surrender to a higher source in order to allow the higher consciousness to move into your being. The essence of real worship is surrender to a higher source, a higher calling.

It may seem that winning and being aggressive are important yet the receptivity of surrendering and obeying are just as important and are vital for soul growth.

Fear keeps people from surrendering to their inner soul urge and subconscious purpose. However, love, LIGHT and truth transform the darkness of fear into the LIGHT of awareness.

Surrendered people have surrendered their conscious ego, which is the devil. Therefore, they are more able to live according to the dictates of I AM.

When you have surrendered your conscious ego you don't have to defend yourself. When there is surrender there is no more fighting. Therefore, you don't need to defend yourself. Also you don't need to offend others.

Jesus surrendered to God's will before the crucifixion when he said, "Not my will but Thy will be done." *Matthew 26:39-43.*

When you surrender your conscious ego-devil you experience peace and then you can experience freedom.

During times of war, freedoms in countries are curtailed. In contrast, in peaceful countries, the people have freedom to create.

Great Christians often think repeatedly of God, or Jesus who became the Christ. Therefore, by imaging your Self as becoming a Christ you move closer to making it a reality "for as you think, so you become."

As you think so you become.

To become closer to God you must practice honesty, says the *Bible*.

The scientific reason why this is so is that in order to align with truth, one must practice honesty and in order to know the Universal Truths one must practice truth in the life. In order to understand the Universal Laws of Creation, one must practice the Universal Truths.

Do not practice hatred, resentment, bitterness, jealousy or revenge, for these keep you in the past. Therefore, they are a barrier to friendship with God and being in the eternal now.

When you release your anger, hate, or resentment and share and reveal your feelings you can begin to heal.

Healing is essentially moving from the past and into the present.

If you have doubts then express them openly and ask for help from God and others.

It is in the practice of the little things, day to day, that determine our ultimate success or failure in life. It is the little disciplines, the little purposes repeated day after day that lead to the real success in life which is enlightenment. It is the little purposes practiced day by day every day that lead to the ultimate fulfillment of one's life purpose.

You can't just be a loner and serve God, for a person who helps and teaches many people comes to know all aspects of Self. Thereby such a one comes to know Self as a creator, made in the image and likeness of God.

Just as your friendships are tested by physical distance or separation so are your friendships with your own inner divinity. Just as it is important for you to have a still mind and be in the present it is also important to realize that God is always present in the now.

Therefore, we can be connected with the High Self, I AM, and God anytime we choose to still the mind and experience what exists in the present moment.

Be willing to say your feelings out loud to yourself and to others for the emotions are the gateway to the heart. And the heart is the gateway to understanding and soul learning. Your thoughts determine your emotions and both determine the way you act.

God's son, Jesus, died for you says some Christian teaching. But what is a religion that is based on death?

Doesn't it make more sense that Jesus who became the enlightened Christ <u>lived for us</u> and lived so we would overcome our mistakes or sins? A sin is a mistake.

Jesus lived for us even more than he died for us.

Enlightened teachers live in order that they can be an example to us and can teach us the power of purpose and having a still mind.

What is the purpose or personal benefit for building and having a still mind? So you can completely receive everything the present moment has to offer you.

The Creator needs us to achieve compatibility in order for the Creator to receive the full benefit of creation. Anyone that creates anything wants his or her creation to mature and reach completion or fulfillment.

Not only is it important to believe that you can attain Christ consciousness, it is also important to build that knowing quality within yourself.

Without love, life doesn't seem much like living.

Without truth, life doesn't seem much like living.

This is because love and truth are the two factors of LIGHT and creation.

Love = the Receptive Principle = Yin

Truth = the Aggressive Principle = Yang.

Yin and Yang are Chinese terms that indicate the receptive and aggressive principles of Creation. I wrote about this in my book, The Tao Te Ching, Interpreted and Explained. Learn to increase your ability to love. Learn to love unselfishly.

Learning to love people and all of life makes all of life much more purposeful. Love is permanent and lasting.

One of the greatest gifts you can give someone is your time and attention. What you are really giving those people is you in the now.

When you are really giving a person or people your whole attention you aren't giving them your time anymore, because you are not in time, you are in the eternal now. There can only be physical time when there is a past and a future. In the eternal now there is neither.

The more we give of ourselves in the present, the more

we live the essence of love.

Whenever you give of your attention to someone you are sacrificing your ego because your ego would like to be in self indulgence.

In order to live the <u>Bible</u> or Christianity it is important to participate in some kind of spiritual group — a place where a person can practice and apply the spiritual or whole mind principles in the life with others.

In my book <u>Permanent Healing</u>, I explain how attitudes affect the physical body and how people can help each other to heal. And how people can use the disorders and disease of their body as a teacher to help them identify their own limiting attitudes. It is important that you live a life of love, truth and LIGHT. A group need not be perfect. There may not be such a thing. There are people in groups and organizations that are trying to learn and grow. Don't wait for things to be perfect before you act or you may be waiting forever.

We only grow by stretching, reaching and taking risks. Sometimes the greatest risk is changing. This is because change involves letting go of our limitations.

Sometimes people talk to me about not being comfortable with this or that change. I tell them comfortableness never caused soul growth and spiritual development. Comfortableness never caused growthful change.

A child is not comfortable learning to walk, crawl or talk, yet they do it. Therefore, to base your learning and growth on comfortableness will only restrict and limit the opportunities available for Self transformation. We grow by taking risks.

As you grow into a whole functioning Self you become more loving, humble, caring and kind.

Remember you can only grow in the present.

Therefore, do not hold onto old grudges, angers, bitterness or hatreds because those attitudes keep a person locked into the past. Holding onto grudges from the past destroys friendships.

Whenever you are hurt by someone, you have a choice to either use it for your learning or to hold onto the past, thereby entrapping yourself.

Humility helps one's learning in all situations.

Wisdom comes in seeing the perspective of others.

Consider that life on Earth is meant to be difficult, not easy. For it is in reaching and stretching that we grow.

There are three parts to the trinity in Christianity — the Father, the Son and the Holy Spirit. The Holy Spirit is the whole Mind. The Father is the Superconscious Mind or I AM. The son is the aggressive conscious mind. The son is the effort of the conscious mind. The whole Mind connects the Father and Son.

Soul growth and Spiritual development require effort. It requires a commitment of your whole being. Most people do not want to commit their whole lives to self awareness and understanding because they are not willing to be fully committed to it.

In order to create change in your Self and in your life, you must change your thoughts and attitudes. This is because everything comes from thoughts. You create your life each day based upon your thoughts.

The first step in quickening your inner learning and improving your ability to fulfill your purpose is to improve the way you think. Mental discipline is the tool to accomplish this.

Mental discipline begins with concentration. Concentration is the tool for mastering thought and for gaining a still mind.

When you sin, which is to make a mistake, you must repent, which is to change your mind. To change your mind requires mental discipline and will power.

To grow in understanding and awareness is a process of

replacing the illusion of separateness, which is a lie, with the truth of universal connectedness.

1. First you hear a greater truth.
2. Then you practice and apply that truth.
3. Then you teach the truth.
4. As you teach the truth, the truth becomes yours more and more.

As you read the <u>Bible</u> ask yourself:

1. How can this knowledge help me fulfill my purpose?
2. How is this teaching universal?
3. How can I apply this teaching?

When a difficult situation arises, ask yourself, "What is the essence of the learning here?"

You grow in enlightenment when you choose the truth-filled life, even when you are tempted to do the exact opposite.

The more enlightened you become, the more your conscious ego-satan will work to try to get you back to being physically engrossed in sensory experiences.

Sometimes, while praying or meditating, an unproductive thought will come to you. When this occurs immediately direct your attention once again to the LIGHT, the brow chakra or to God.

Avoidance of an unproductive thought does not make it go away. Avoidance only drives the thought deeper in your unconscious.

When the unproductive thought arises then observe it, admit it is there and redirect your attention to where it needs to be. Continually focus your attention on LIGHT, Love and Truth and you will become LIGHT, Love and Truth.

You must gain control of your mind in order to gain control of yourself. Sometimes it feels like a battle, yet it is a battle you can win. It requires discipline and a strong purpose. Do not dwell on unproductive thoughts. Instead separate them out and identify them. Admit they are yours. Then reconnect with the true reality. Replace the limited or unproductive thought with a more truth-filled thought.

Find a church or organization where the people genuinely care for each other. Love must be present in order for the truth of understanding and wisdom to flourish. When there is love, many people will come to be a part of what is being created.

Associate with people that help you to elevate your thoughts. Move away from those that would have you lower your consciousness. Think regularly about enlightened beings such as Jesus the Christ to help you resist temptation and to move your consciousness forward.

When someone opens up and shares their thoughts and feelings about themselves I am glad because I know that person is ready to move forward in soul growth and spiritual development. I keep teaching and offering the learning, knowledge, wisdom and understanding I have gained. If you want to keep growing, the best way to learn more is to pass on what you have already learned.

Thought to remember:

You are an eternal I AM. You are not just a physical body. Still the mind and know I AM in the present moment.

Exercise to practice:

Read the Bible every day. Be disciplined about this. Read other Holy Books such as The Bhagavad Gita, the Dhammapada and the Tao Te Ching to compare them to the Bible .

Chapter 21
Kundalini, Creative Energy and Purpose

It is important to create purpose. Therefore, this chapter will present instruction concerning the creative energy and how to use it in relation to purpose.

It is important to be aware that there are two ways of being that can be accessed for creating. One of these factors most people are familiar with. It is called imagination. Many people do not use imagination effectively while some do. Imagination is also called imaging or visualization.

The second factor is called Kundalini. Kundalini is a word from India that means serpent fire. The Kundalini energy is like a fire in that heat can be felt in the physical body when the Kundalini rises.

Kundalini energy is also like a fire in that when aroused it can burn out limitations or restrictions in the physical body as well as mentally and emotionally.

The Kundalini can be used to aid in the raising of one's consciousness when it rises from its resting place at the base of the spine. As it rises, the Kundalini, serpent fire energy enlivens the seven chakras which are located in the area of the ductless glands of the body.

The word *chakra*, from India, literally means wheel. The chakras are energy transformers that recycle used mental energy back into the higher divisions of mind. These higher divisions are the subconscious and superconscious minds.

Everyone has chakras. Most are functioning below capacity.

As one reaches for higher purpose in life and holds in mind high ideals of enlightenment, awareness or spiritual being, the Kundalini is aroused.

It then rises up the spine and out the crown of the head. As it rises, it touches, penetrates and moves through each of the seven chakras.

The Kundalini energy starts out at the base of the spine when it touches and vivifies the root chakra. Then it continues its climb up the spinal column touching and moving through the spleen chakra, the solar plexus chakra, the heart chakra, the throat chakra, the brow chakra or third eye, and finally the crown chakra located above the crown of the head.

As the Kundalini rises, one experiences a heightened awareness and an elevation of consciousness. After the experience, the Kundalini may return to the base of the spine leaving one with a sense of awe and wonder over what has been achieved.

Once this happens you will never be the same again. Your consciousness may gradually drift back to a position close to where it was before, yet you will never be quite the same.

It is an experience of expanded consciousness that one can neither deny nor avoid. It was real. What you are left with is a desire for more. What remains is a burning desire to reach the heights of consciousness and fulfillment permanently that you experienced temporarily.

This heightened consciousness is of permanent benefit. Therefore, it has great and lasting purpose.

What is the greatest purpose? In other words, what is the greatest benefit? It is cosmic consciousness. It is Christ consciousness. It is Buddha consciousness. It is to be embraced in the Creator's all encompassing love. It is of the greatest benefit to experience as Jesus the Christ proclaimed, "I and the Father are one."

Oneness is unity consciousness. It is the full connectedness of being with Self and all creation. It is the full alignment of
conscious and subconscious minds and attunement to
Superconscious Mind. It is knowing Self as I AM existing beyond time, space and vibratory creation.

The raising of the Kundalini creative energy enables one
to experience the next evolutionary stage of development of humanity and human beings.

Most people are not even aware that Kundalini energy
exists. A few know it exists and is a reality. More are waking up
to the reality of Kundalini energy and its potential to aid each
individual to know Self and all creation.

The Kundalini energy in relation to the chakras is referred
to in the Bible , *Book of Revelation*. The seven churches in Asia
referred to in Revelation chapters two and three symbolize the
seven chakras.

The message written to each church in Asia in the *Book of
Revelation* is instruction concerning the proper use and development of the chakras.

Chapter 22 of *Revelation* refers to a pure river of the water
of the Life. (*Revelation* 22:1). This pure River of the water of Life
is the Kundalini energy.

The writer or writers of the *Bible, Book of Revelation* understood the Kundalini energy and wished to convey their knowledge to those with eyes to see.

People throughout history have had experiences of
Kundalini energy and have, through this, discovered a higher
purpose of life, a higher state of being.

Some of these enlightened masters have written of this
higher purpose and this higher state of consciousness. Some of
these writings may be found in the Holy Books of the world.

What in the past was a matter of believing, not believing
or unawareness is now becoming more and more known.

I have had the experience of the opening of all seven

chakras. I have had the experience of my Kundalini, creative energy rising up from the base of my spine all the way through the chakras up to and beyond the top of my head and through the crown chakra.

My life has never been the same since, and your life will never be the same either once you have experienced the power of the full Kundalini energy.

Visualization pales in comparison to the full power of the Kundalini energy. Although visualization is a helpful aid in learning to use the mind productively and to thereby prepare to receive the glory of the Kundalini energy.

Once the Kundalini is experienced fully, you live a higher purpose based on a higher knowledge, a higher consciousness and a higher awareness.

What is that higher purpose? What is that higher life that the human being, the individual, can live while still existing in a physical body in the physical world?

This higher purpose is the awareness and consciousness of the oneness, the full connectedness of all creation. This is the full awareness experience that you are not separate, you are not alone and your purpose is intimately connected to a larger, greater purpose that involves all humanity and indeed the entire universe.

What is the difference between an enlightened being and an ordinary mortal? The ordinary or average human being perceives wrongly the Self as separate from the world and everyone in it. The senses seem to verify this distance or space between people, places and things. However, it is an illusion.

The enlightened being knows from direct perception and experience the connectedness of all creation. Therefore, the basis upon which the enlightened being thinks, acts and exists is very different from the basis upon which the average thinker or human being exists.

This leads to a totally different perspective on life and a

totally different set of priorities for the life.

The one who views life as separate has a purpose of protection and accumulation of physical things. Such a one usually holds some fear in mind.

The one who knows life to be connected and of a whole unity lives a life based on the connectedness of love, LIGHT, and truth.

Such a one lives the adage "do unto others as you would have them do unto you" because it is based on the scientific reality of the connectedness of all beings.

Therefore, as you aid another you benefit yourself. As you harm another you harm yourself.

The Kundalini energy teaches the lesson of Love, LIGHT, truth and connectedness. It is available for all who would practice these basic principles.

Thought to remember:

I am a creator. I create greater LIGHT, awareness and understanding in myself every day.

What to do:

Seek a teacher that can teach you to concentrate, meditate, breathe life force and raise the Kundalini.

Chapter 22
Karma and Purpose
Learning the Universal Lessons of Life
Karma Explained

1. Karma is indebtedness as an individual.
2. Karma is created by intention.
3. Karma is relieved by understanding.

The debt you owe to yourself as an individual is to build the full understanding of Self as a creator. You are to become an enlightened being, a son of God.

Any limitation in consciousness tends to create karma. Therefore, create thoughts of helping others and helping yourself improve every day. Learn the Universal Laws and Universal Truths of Life and live by them.

Karma is a physical manifestation of the Universal Law of Cause and Effect. Karma brings the lessons of life to you in physical ways in order to learn the mental or higher truths.

Karma is relieved by understanding the lesson you need to learn in order to be more in harmony with the true nature of reality, which is connectedness.

Karma is the Universal Lesson of Life that is coming at you. Karma brings the repeated experiences that you create or have over and over again until you learn the lesson. Karma shows up in the way one keeps drawing the same type of people to the Self. Karma is apparent in the way one draws similar situations and circumstances to the Self.

Once the Universal Lesson of Life is received into the Self and thereby learned then one's life, situations and circumstances change. The quality of one's life improves. You find yourself associating with people whose thoughts and attitudes are more in alignment with Universal Law and Universal Truth.

When you identify a limitation in consciousness, rejoice because you have earned the right to receive that Universal Lesson of Life that has come to you.

Permanent understandings always align with and are in accord with Universal Laws and Universal Truths.

All wrong thinking, all false or erroneous beliefs, eventually fall away and are replaced with the permanent understanding of Self and creation that is called en-LIGHT-en-ment.

When you identify a limitation in consciousness, rejoice because that means you are capable of learning the Universal Lesson of Life right now in the present. You are capable of receiving the karma-learning, the Universal Life Lesson and the understanding into the Self.

As one learns these Universal Life Lessons, one's Self value increases.

There are a lot of people with low Self value. There is a way to build greater Self value and people need to know how to do it. Every time you build understanding of Self and Mind, you understand and know your value to a greater degree. Low Self worth is a detriment to soul growth and spiritual development. Low Self worth is a bottleneck, a limitation in consciousness.

Every time you receive new awareness into yourself, you gain value. Awareness is valuable. Using awareness to build wisdom and understanding is even more valuable. Using the awareness, understanding and wisdom to receive enlightenment is of the highest value.

Humbleness

The greater the Self value, the greater the capability for humbleness.

The greater the inner security, the greater the opportunity for humbleness.

The greater the enlightenment, the greater the opportunity for humbleness.

So never image or visualize or imagine yourself as being unworthy, unloved or valueless. To develop true humbleness you must have great Self value.

True humbleness means to use your ego correctly and productively for yourself and for others in the best way possible. Do this in the best way you know how until you learn how to do it better.

Humbleness is a surrendered ego that is willing to learn.

In order to have a productive ego one must realize the interconnectedness of all beings and all of creation.

The true nature of reality is connectedness.

Therefore, the phrase "do unto others as you would have them do unto you" is a scientific principle that explains how to harmonize with the true nature of reality to promote one's own betterment.

Because the purpose of our existence in physical life and the physical body is to move toward and grow into enlightenment, a productive ego is one that motivates us forward to enlightenment.

One who is using the ego productively continually adds to the Self in wisdom, understanding and awareness while aiding others to do the same.

True humbleness is indicated in one who can ask questions and listen with a still mind.

The word *education* means to draw forth or bring forth. Therefore, one who asks questions and listens is able to draw forth knowledge and learning in every situation thereby educating the Self.

It is not always easy to still your mind in order to receive completely what the other person has to say. Nevertheless, stilling the mind is a good exercise for disciplining of the mind and conscious ego.

Stilling the mind and listening helps to bring about a balance of the aggressive and receptive qualities of the Self so that one is no longer at the mercy of the pairs of opposites which are the extremes of physical existence.

The pairs of opposites are the extremes of physical existence such as good and bad, right and wrong, black and white, hot and cold.

The more one leaves the mind undisciplined the more one's mind goes to extremes. From this the individual is either happy or sad but rarely, if ever, fulfilled.

Fulfillment is a function of a still mind.

Mind is the vehicle to know the Self.

Therefore, an undisciplined mind will never know the Real Self and will never know the great fulfillment.

An undisciplined mind will spend years and even a lifetime engrossed, entrenched and caught up in physical, sensory experiences never realizing there is something greater than temporary sensory gratification.

The conscious ego or the egotistical person will want to

have the last say, or prove they are right, to talk the loudest, or the most or always get their way.

How will you know the needs of another if you don't listen? Listening is how one person can become aware of the needs of another.

Listening requires a still mind.

Listening is a function of receptivity. Listening is the ability to receive with the mind. Therefore, cultivate the ability to listen with an open mind and an open heart. Have no other thoughts in your mind while listening to another.

It is in cultivating the ability to receive that one will learn to receive with awareness their purpose in life from their inner, subconscious mind.

In order to learn in any experience you need to receive that experience. Any thoughts or anything that impedes one's ability to listen and receive must be separated out, identified, admitted and replaced with the still mind and thoughts of connectedness.

It is a good practice to identify one's limitations in consciousness. It is a productive practice to identify areas of low Self worth, or feelings of inadequacy or incapability. It is productive to identify any negative thinking about Self that is not in alignment with Universal Laws and Universal Truths. It is productive to identify limiting thoughts and attitudes in order that they may be replaced with more productive, valuable thoughts concerning the Self and others.

It has been said that nature abhors a void. Therefore, if you try to remove a thought of blame you must replace it with a thought of gratitude. Replace hate with love and anger with openness in order to learn the lessons of life.

In this way, one comes to live a higher purpose.

In order to choose a different thought one must identify

the thought one holds in the brain or conscious mind. By saying the thought out loud one comes to know the thought. By knowing the thought, one can come to realize that **what you do to yourself you usually do to other people.**

What you think in your silent thoughts or your loud thoughts of yourself you usually do to other people because that is your consciousness. How could it be otherwise? That is your consciousness.

How can you be something for someone that you are not?

The purpose of life is not negative or hateful, and your purpose for this life is not negative, restrictive or limiting. In fact, the purpose of life is all-encompassing. It is specifically designed to add to one's consciousness.

The purpose of life is an individual's way of adding to their sum total of knowledge, wisdom and understanding.

The purpose of communication is to arrive at a greater truth.

The purpose of communication is not to determine who is right and who is wrong.

Have a purpose for listening. Listen for what you can add to yourself, your awareness, and your consciousness. One who has a still mind can receive anything. People who live in fear are not open to receive. They are afraid of being hurt. The individual must become so centered in Self awareness and Self knowing that one remains open. Then one is able to learn, receive, flower and grow at all times, in all situations.

Receive and thereby add to the Self. By being open, one receives. By receiving, one learns to give.

A still mind can receive. A still mind is receptive. A still mind is an open mind.

Included in this chapter is a Past Life-Karma intuitive report given at the School of Metaphysics. This intuitive report was given by a conductor and intuitive reporter team that had trained and practiced developing their minds for years.

What is a conductor?

A conductor is a person that trains intuitive reporters. A conductor directs intuitive reports.

What is an intuitive reporter?

An intuitive reporter is an individual that is trained by a conductor so that together they may offer intuitive reports to the public.

What kind of intuitive reports?

The main Intuitive Reports offered by the School of Metaphysics are Past Life-Karma Reports, Past Life Crossings between two people, and Health Analyses. A Health Analysis determines one's mental, emotional and physical condition.

Other Intuitive Reports, such as Dharma Reports, Transference of Energy Reports and Creative Mind Reports, are offered to students and to individuals attending weekend Spiritual Focus Sessions on the College of Metaphysics Campus.

Karma and Purpose

Karma is a bond that forms after one's consciousness has chosen to settle into a certain way.

This settling of consciousness creates a learning pattern that is repeated over and over that is an attempt to connect the inner and outer mind.

Connecting the inner and outer mind enables the thinker to become aware of a part of creation that can be put into a form of an understanding of Self and creation. Karma is not bad. Karma is necessary at this point of humanity's journey in fulfilling the purpose of life. It is part of the learning in order that one can become more Self aware and fulfilled.

The following is a past life profile given at the School of Metaphysics. The first part of the intuitive report describes a past life for the individual requesting the intuitive report. In this case, the past life time took place in Ireland.

The second part of the intuitive report is what is of most interest in this chapter. The second part relates the significance of that past life to the present life for this individual. This significance is the karma of this person in the present time period.

By using and applying the significance, which is the knowledge of one's karma, the lesson of life may be learned. The karma of this individual may be relieved and fulfilled much more rapidly.

Conductor: You will search for the identity of the entity referred to as _____ and relate a significant incarnation for this entity.

> *Intuitive Reporter: We see this one in female form. We see for this to be in a land area known as Ireland. We see that this was during a time where there was great hardship amongst the people. We see that there was very little food for the masses, and there were few who were wealthy that monopolized this country at this time. We see that this one was in a family that was very poor, and we see that all of the children were malnourished. We see that the ones of the parents recognized this and did give the children to different wealthy families as servants. We see that this was an act of love on the parents part because they believed that this was the only way the children would be provided for. We see that this one did not understand this at this time and was extremely emotional about the separation from her family. We see that she was completely withdrawn and depressed for a*

number of weeks when she was left. We see that the wife in this household was quite compassionate and did reach out to this one to nurture this one. We see although this one was brought into the home in the capacity of a servant, it was generosity upon the part of the family in wanting to aid as many people as they could that they brought this one in. Therefore, this one was accepted, mainly as part of the family. We see that there were certain duties that were expected of this one that this one did do, did accomplish, however this one was also included in all of the family activities. We see that this one warmed to this and did open up, and we do see that this one embraced the opportunity and used the opportunity for education, for culture. For we do see that this one believed that this was how this one would be able to get back to her own parents. And we see that this one wanted very much to marry well and to provide for the ones of the parents, through a well-placed marriage. We see that this was arranged, and we do see that this one married into a great deal of money, and we see that it was easy for this one to accept this because this one used her money to aid other people. We see that a kind of orphanage or kind of shelter was built that this one inspired and this one did run. And we see that this one did serve and reach many, many people of all ages within her community. We see for this one, herself, to raise four children. And we see that the eldest of these children died unexpectantly when this one was injured and this was heart-breaking to this one. We see that this did renew this one's vigor to aid as many people as possible and this is what moved this one to do this. We see for this one to continue in this capacity throughout this one's life. We see for this one to live to be eighty-two years old. We see for this one to be called Erin Lofk.

Conductor: Very well, what would be the significance of that lifetime to the present lifetime for this entity?

> *Intuitive Reporter: We see that at the present time there is vision that this one does have of how this one wants to give, and we see that this one is actively pursuing this vision. We do see, however, that there are patterns of thinking that this one does have that interfere with this one realizing this one's vision. Would suggest to this one to be willing to identify these patterns of thinking, for we see in this area this one tends to be vague with the self. We see at times this one uses humor. We see that this one uses sarcasm to cover these patterns or in essence to deny the awareness to the self of this. We see that this only hurts the self and limits this one's capacity to give. Would suggest to this one to be willing to embrace change, to rely on faith and act on this one's vision. For the most part, it is when this one falls short of action that this one stays stuck, for there is a passivity and a laziness that this one lets take over. This is an example of the patterns of thinking that has been described. This one is well aware of what this one needs to do. It is a matter of this one matching will with desire. This is all. (3-5-2000-CAA-DRC-5)*

This intuitive report given relates a past lifetime in Ireland.

More importantly, in the second part of the Intuitive Report, wisdom and knowledge are given to aid this person to clearly see the next step in fulfilling karma.

In order to fulfill her karma, this person needs to identify habitual thinking and patterns of thinking that interfere with the fulfillment of her vision.

This one also needs to match will with her desire. She

needs to develop will power.

As a disciplined mind is developed, the thoughts one has become more apparent. People tend to be unconscious of many of their thoughts until the mind is disciplined through the effort of will. This intuitive report relates the karma of this individual.

The first step to causing a change is being aware of the change you need to make.

The first step to learning a subject is to begin to educate yourself concerning that subject.

In order to fulfill your karma at a more rapid rate, you will need to learn and understand your karma.

The best way I know to be aware of your karma clearly, and thereby relieve it, is to receive a past life Intuitive Report with its significance from the School of Metaphysics. The significance, or second part of the Intuitive Report, is your karma at the time you received this Intuitive Report.

How many people on this planet know their karma? Not many.

What percentage of the people on this planet know their karma? Less than one percent!

By the time students have reached lesson nine in the course of study at the School of Metaphysics, they have received a past life Intuitive Report from the School of Metaphysics. These students have knowledge of their karma.

This information, knowledge, and wisdom concerning one's karma is invaluable to the individual.

Knowing your karma helps you to know your purpose.

How does knowing your karma help you to know your purpose? Karma is: indebtedness as an individual. The debt you owe to yourself is that of knowing the Self.

To know the Self means not only to be aware of one's habits, fears or ways of thinking. To know the Self is to use one's mind to create the enlightened Self. Then one arrives at the point or place beyond thought that is being or consciousness itself.

One's purpose is found in knowing the Self as a creator. Your purpose on Earth is fulfilled by coming to know who you are as an eternal being.

Karma is the Universal lesson or lessons of life that keep coming at you. You owe it to yourself to learn these lessons of life. Karma affords just the learning each individual needs to find the universal truths and to discover all the many aspects of the Self.

Have you ever asked yourself why you keep re-acting over and over to the same kind of people, or why you create the same type of job situations over and over again? There is a universal lesson of life that you need to receive into yourself.

That is why the same lesson seems to come up, over and over in different areas of your life.

The lesson needed to be learned is Universal in your life!

Karma brings these Universal Lessons to us until they are learned.

To learn the lesson:

1. Make the lesson a part of the Self.
2. Incorporate the Universal Lesson into one's being.
3. Transform one's consciousness.
4. Add to one's mind in such a way that one will never go back to the old, limited way of thinking.
5. Become a better and wiser person.
6. Grow in love, LIGHT, and Truth.
7. Expand your awareness and consciousness,
8. Be more connected with all of life, all beings and all of the universe.

To fulfill your purpose in life you must learn the lessons needed. Karma brings those lessons to you. You must be willing to receive these Universal Life Lessons.

Most people physicalize these lessons as they blame others for their problems, re-actions and limitations in life. It is victim consciousness. Victim consciousness is based on the wrong thinking and false perception that everything in life is separated and disconnected. If everything is separate and disconnected, then your experiences and lessons of life are separated from everyone and everything else.

This is the great illusion. Separateness is the great illusion.

The true nature of reality is connectedness.

Therefore, your lessons in life, your experiences, are directly related to your thoughts, your attitudes, your feelings, your choices and your actions.

Your choices in life have brought you or led you to your present life circumstances and conditions. If you want something different in life then make different choices. In order to make different choices, you will need to discipline your mind. To discipline the mind you will need to practice concentration exercises and meditate every day.

When concentration and meditation are practiced every day, awareness of one's thoughts is achieved. Being aware of your thoughts you may weed out the limiting thoughts, such as anger, hatred, fear, revenge, jealousy, deceit, manipulation, greed, abuse and resentment.

Unproductive thoughts may be replaced with love, truth and LIGHT filled thoughts of universal connectedness.

The physical senses give us the illusion that we are separate and alone and therefore, powerless. After all, isn't there physical distance between one person and another?

This is the great illusion, for we are all connected. Quantum physics has proven this over and over in experiments that help show that the experimenter affects the experiments.

Enlightened masters throughout the ages have proclaimed the truth of universal connectedness.

This is why the command of Jesus, the enlightened, to do unto others as you would have them do unto you is a scientifically valid principle. Because of the reality of universal connectedness, the way you treat others is what the Universe and Universal Subconscious Mind always returns to you.

Therefore, the Universal Lessons of Life always have to do with recognizing the true nature of reality which is connectedness. Relieving your karma always indicates living less under the illusion of separateness and more in the truth of connectedness.

Fulfilling your purpose in life always involves living more in the truth of connectedness and bringing your consciousness into the being of Universal Oneness.

Thought to remember:

You draw situations, circumstances and experiences to yourself for the universal life lessons and for the fulfillment of karma.

What to do:

While in your life situations, ask yourself, "How did I draw this experience to me and how did I create this experience?"

Chapter 23
Dharma and Purpose

Dharma is a word from India that means duty.

When people consider duty, they may think of a soldier who does his duty and helps win the battle or dies trying. This may be an example of physical duty, yet this is another kind of duty. This other kind of duty, this higher duty, is to the soul or subconscious mind. Dharma is your mission to serve, give to or teach the world.

Each of these chapters in this book give you insight into purpose. Dharma is not purpose, yet fulfilling your dharma helps you to understand and realize your purpose.

Dharma is what you have and need to give to the world. It is your duty to give to the world. Everyone needs to give to others. The Earth was here before we came into the world. Therefore, it is our duty to give back to the world. When you were born you were given to and nourished. You were clothed, fed, protected, sheltered, cared for and usually loved. You were given to, and as a baby, you received. You absorbed and received and matured rapidly.

As you matured through infancy to adolescence, you became more responsible. As you progressed from adolescence to adulthood, you became fully responsible for your self. If you matured, it was because you were taught correctly and productively. Then you were able to function in the world productively and responsibly.

I have discovered that the hallmark of adulthood as a reasoner is to produce more than you consume. There are a lot of people in the world that produce less than they consume. It is our duty to help others to live a more fulfilling and productive life.

It is also by producing more than you consume that you are able to move into the fourth stage of growth, wisdom.

Wisdom is the stage of growth achieved when one teaches others what has been learned and the students become teachers to more students. Thus, the learning becomes continual and connected.

Everyone has a dharma in the world because it is everyone's duty to give to the world.

Usually people are the happiest and most satisfied when they are giving. It is in giving that we are open to receive. It is in giving that we recognize our value, importance and worth.

Truly great people recognize their worth and value through what they offer and give each day.

Some people are recognized for what they give. Others go unrecognized except to a very few. Sometimes the greatest givers aren't even well known or famous.

What do you want or have or need to give to the world? It starts with what is right in front of you. You start by giving to those around and near you.

I like to grow an organic garden because I enjoy teaching students how to apply and live in harmony with the Universal Laws and nature. Raising young plants that are full of life and vitality reminds one that life is for living and giving.

To aid a young cabbage plant to grow and mature teaches us, among other things, that we have life energy to give to others.

As I teach my students to water a row of kale they learn that when they give there is growth.

As I teach students to weed a row of tomatoes, I notice they appreciate and enjoy the tomatoes they receive from those plants much more than they would if they hadn't cared for the plants.

You gain value in what you give to.

Some people give a lot, some a little. A few give their all.

World teachers and world saviors give their all. Sometimes people give their all and yet do not become famous. Famousness is not necessarily a gauge of one's givingness, nor of one's dharma fulfillment.

What is important is that you discover what you have to give to the world. To one degree or another it is always uniquely yours. Even if you give what someone else is giving, it still will have your unique individuality and experience.

Do you think your life's purpose is to work on a factory production line? Do you think you are here to do mindless repetitive work? Do you think that is your duty?

Your duty is in service. Your dharma is in giving. How does a person discover what he or she has to give? The answer is by giving.

Get involved in a church or service organization. Find out how you can serve your community. Notice what kinds of learning you are drawn to. Investigate to discover where your true interests lie. Once you have discovered your major interest in life, then give it your best.

Fortunate is the one whose desire to do and desire to give coincide.

Some people have a job. While at that job they work for a person or a company. Then on weekends they attend a service organization, church or other place of giving.

Some people only give of their money. Money is a means of exchange, a way to transfer value. Yet the greatest value is your time, attention and effort. Your real essence, the Real you that resides inside, is of the greatest value. This is the essence of what you have to give to the world.

People so often hold back on giving of themselves because of the fear of not being good enough or not having anything valuable to say.

One of the things I have always taught my son, Hezekiah, is that what he has to say is important. The primary way I teach him this is by giving him my full attention when he has something he wants to tell me. Even when I am talking with adults, if Kie wants to talk to me, I stop what I am doing to listen to what he has to say. My son is valuable and important.

Children know they are valuable and important until taught otherwise by adults who refuse to give them their full attention often.

The old adage "children are to be seen, not heard" is simply wrong thinking. Childhood is the time we most need both quantity and quality time. In this way, the child's innate sense of value is reinforced. That value then manifests itself as the willingness and joy in giving and receiving as an adult.

Children have a sense of their destiny. This sense, this openness, can remain in the child's awareness as she or he matures. Factory or government schools have a cookie cutter approach to indoctrination, otherwise known as public education.

Each child is a unique individual with unique attributes, unique understanding, unique learning and a unique Dharma to give to the world.

Yet there are also universals that each child needs. Each child needs love, caring, kindness, softness, gentleness, nurturing and teaching. The child's first teachers are the parents. The parents are meant to be the main teachers throughout childhood. Yet all too often, the teachers of the children are the baby sitters, the day care adults or the grade school teachers.

In order to lead a fulfilling life, one must fulfill the destiny, the duty, the Dharma.

The games you played when you were a child will tell you a lot about what you are to be doing as an adult.

Children know much more than you may think. The life essence that chooses to use the baby's body is very intelligent and holds much permanent learning and understanding. Therefore, encourage the child in his interests. Encourage yourself in your interests also. Once you have discovered your passion in life, then live it with the full commitment.

When you are fully committed, wonderful things begin to happen. When fully committed to fulfilling your Dharma, your life takes on greater meaning and value. You are fulfilling your inner urge in the present.

The following is a Dharma report given by myself as Conductor and my wife, Barbara, as Intuitive Reporter.

Usually in Dharma Intuitive Reports, a key word is given in the first sentence or two that describes one's Dharma.

This is incredible when you consider that fewer than one percent of the people on the planet know their Dharma. Most don't even know what Dharma is.

In the sample Intuitive Report given, the person's Dharma is given as devotion. Just knowing that your life revolves around or focuses on Dharma makes for a tremendously more fulfilling life.

Conductor: You will search for the identity of the entity referred to as _____ and you will relate this one's dharma from the past and past lifetimes in general in terms of incarnations.

Intuitive Reporter: This is devotion. We see that there have been many opportunities for this one to learn the value of persistence and the value of commitment. We see that these have come in a variety of forms to this one and there have been as many opportunities that this one has wasted or cast aside. We see that the times of the greatest movement and the greatest bringing of under-

standing into the Self have been in positions where this one was affiliated with some kind of religious study. We see that there have been many incarnations where this one has been either a monk or a nun in some form of religious study and we see that it is during these times where this one can immerse the Self in devotion and can begin to cause there to be a catharsis of understanding within the Self.

We see that it is a very strong urge within this one to be faithful and we see that the greatest temptations that this one experiences in life is from a movement away from this. We see that the aggregate amount of experience, however, that has brought into this one, the kind of understanding that is necessary of a dharma, has been brought to bear within the present and we see, therefore, there is a very strong inner urge that this one has toward that of spiritual development and the openness to being able to cause it to come forward. It would be most helpful to this one to honor this and to develop it to a point of respect. This one's greatest challenge in this regard is the same that it has been many different times which is a temptation away from the devotion itself, the dedication of thoughts and actions toward an ideal. This one has had experiences where it has been easy for this one to be distracted and therefore this one has lost the thread of the dharma itself. There have been times when this one was challenged and did not meet the challenge and therefore lost the thread of the dharma. There have been times when this one has been tempted and has moved away but then returned to...with a greater insight into the livingness of the devotion. It is within the present time period that this one is capable of causing there to be a conscious integration of this in the con-

sciousness itself. Discipline is the means by which this can expect to be brought to the Self. It would be helpful for this one to embody the meaning of religious. This is all.

Conductor: This entity says, "How can I best use my dharma in relation to teaching?"

Intuitive Reporter: This would become apparent in the love that this one is capable of giving to others. It is in this that the motivations can be uplifted and can be illumined with the quality that devotion is. (2-2-2002-BGC-DRC-2)

Discipline of the mind is required for fulfilling fully one's dharma.

This person's dharma is given as devotion. Dedication of thoughts and actions toward an ideal are what produce devotion.

Persistence and commitment are also important qualities in the fulfillment of the dharma. Openness and faithfulness are important qualities that aid and allow anyone's dharma to come forward.

In order to fully give to the world the understanding and knowledge you are here to give there must be a commitment to stick to your ideals in order to fulfill them fully. Once you have decided what you want to achieve and give to humanity, be persistent and disciplined in doing so. Be open to receive the continual learning that comes to one who pursues their inner urge.

Your dharma is to be used to create in the day-to-day life for the purpose of learning to understand the process of creating and creation.

You are here on mother Earth to learn to create. In fulfilling the dharma one not only learns the process of creation, one also teaches this process to others.

Thought to remember:
     You have something valuable to give to the world.

What to do:
     Identify your strengths and interests. Develop and give
these.

Chapter 24
Breath and Purpose

Everyone breathes. Everyone that lives in a physical body breathes. Breath is the factor that binds the soul to the physical body.

A human being is dependent on air to sustain the body. More than food, more than water, air is indispensable for existence in a physical body.

Therefore, it would seem that understanding and mastering breath would be of utmost importance to each individual. Yet it is relatively rare for people to learn to use the breath correctly, much less effectively.

In order to have a purpose for physical existence in a physical body, there must be breath and there must be air.

Most people do not understand the connection between breath and purpose. Yet one who practices breath control or breath discipline or breathing exercises or breathwork almost invariably comes to know the purpose of life to a greater degree. Such a one also comes to realize to a much greater degree his or her unique and individual purpose.

Why is this so and how does it work?

Since breath is the factor that binds the soul or subconscious mind to the physical body, it is breath that can aid one to know the soul's or subconscious mind's purpose for incarning into and inhabiting a physical body.

People that do not understand breath often sound like they are drowning as they take in one breath after another in rapid secession. It is as if they are gasping for air.

The one who has practiced breathwork, however, is able to slow the breath down at will. Such a one also tends to breathe at a slower rate than the uneducated breather. This is because as the individual gains greater understanding and mastery of the breath, there is greater efficiency in breathing. This means that whatever air is breathed can be utilized more effectively by the body. Therefore, the efficient, learned breather can actually gain greater benefits with less breaths. The result is the breathing is quieter yet the cells and organs of the body are better fed the oxygen they need.

As one continues to build the will through the conscious choice of breathing, the conscious mind becomes capable of receiving the higher truth, knowledge, and purpose from subconscious mind.

Thus, through breathwork or pranayama as it is known in India, one becomes more attuned to the soul. Since breath is the factor that binds the soul or subconscious mind to the physical body, it becomes of utmost importance to master the breath.

I remember as a child I had difficulty removing my attention from the breath. I couldn't seem to stop watching my breath. As a child I often wanted to play. Sometimes when I was with others and sometimes by myself, it seemed irritating or frustrating at these times that I couldn't seem to stop watching my breath, especially since I wanted to be doing other things.

As an adult having trained my mind and breath, I know this ability to observe the breath to be a permanent understanding, a blessing, or as some might say, a gift.

I look upon this natural ability to observe the breath as a preparation so that in early adult life I would take up the study of Self, mind and breath which is called Metaphysics.

I had built this understanding of breath, attention and concentration and now carried it through to this lifetime.

Each lifetime is an opportunity to build permanent understandings of Self and creation. Each lifetime the soul existing in Subconscious or Universal Mind gains the opportunity to build, through experience, these permanent, eternal and lasting understandings of Self. This soul learning or permanent learning of Self does not happen or occur just because you go through an experience. Otherwise every elderly person on the planet or every person above a certain age on the planet would be enlightened.

It is not just the experience, but the opportunity to draw forth the essence of the learning, the universal learning, in each experience that enables the Self to build and gain permanent understandings of Self and creation.

The key to being able to receive the essence of the learning in every experience is the disciplined use of the mind and attention.

Concentration exercises are the first step to building mastery of the attention. Mastering the ability to hold the attention on the breath gives the ability to go beyond the entrapment of the Self and know the Real Self that exists beyond the physical body.

Breath binds you to the physical body. Therefore, master the breath and you master the body. Master the breath and you master the factor that binds the inner Self to the outer Self. Master the breath and thereby master the ability to know the inner Self, the High Self, the Real Self.

In order to know your purpose in life, the ability to gain perception beyond the five senses is a must. The discipline of the mind and breath gives one the ability to perceive beyond the five senses. This enables one to go where the five senses alone will not take you.

The oxygen in the air feeds the body. Blood carries oxygen throughout the body to feed the cells. What could be more important to the physical body than understanding and enhancing this process?

If you become a more efficient breather then the physical

body's chances of staying healthy may increase. How does one get better at any skill or ability? The answer is attention and practice.

Attention and practice give understanding of purpose in life and of life.

To fulfill your purpose in life you must breathe. Therefore, learn to breathe correctly and productively. This begins by observing the breath. You will notice that as you observe the breath, your breathing begins to become more relaxed and calm.

As the breath becomes more relaxed and calm it is easier for the mind to become still and calm. As the mind and breath become still and calm, one's purpose is received into one's conscious awareness.

When you are drawn to some area of learning, some special interest, realize that this may be the inner mind's way of bringing purpose to you. Your outer life may be connecting with your inner purpose.

People often miss these golden opportunities because the mind is so undisciplined and the attention is scattered. The person whose attention is scattered or racing usually lives with fear. Living in fear, one misses the opportunities of life because one misinterprets the life experiences based on one's own fear.

Fear never gives one an accurate perception of life. Fear colors the experiences while filtering out the LIGHT of truth and awareness.

Students who have practiced breathwork, breathe on average at a slower rate. This is possible because each breath is more fully and efficiently used by the body. When the body is relaxed, less oxygen is required. When the body is running, the runner gasps for air. When the mind is racing, the body re-acts and thinks it is racing. The body then gasps for air.

When the mind is at rest, the body can be at rest. When the mind and body are at rest, the breathing is relaxed, calm and peaceful. The individual can rest even in the day-to-day activities.

Only when the mind and breath are calm can the higher purpose be known.

Thought to remember:
Use the breath purposefully for health and awareness.

What to do:
Observe the breath.

Chapter 25
Teaching Indigo and Crystal Children with Purpose

I was in the pet shop in Lebanon, Missouri with my nine-year-old Indigo son, Hezekiah. Kie loves pets. He had often gone to the pet store with his Mommy, who is my wife Barbara, and myself.

Today Hezekiah and I were at the pet shop looking at fish in the aquariums. There were goldfish as well as tropical fish.

We were enjoying ourselves looking at the fish and Hezekiah was excited about it. He was telling me about the fish.

Then a woman that worked at the pet shop came up to me and asked if she could help us. I said we hadn't decided what we wanted yet.

Then Hezekiah asked the woman a question about why this kind of fish needed a heater for their water. She answered "because that's the way they are."

I knew that was not a real answer, so I explained to Hezekiah why those kind of fish needed a heater for their water. They are tropical fish, and in the tropics the water is always warm.

Indigo and Crystal children are inquisitive and want to learn. They want to know the answers to life. They want to understand the purpose of life and everything about it.

In fact, Indigo and Crystal children already know a lot about the purpose of life! They come into this life with a strong purpose. They choose their purpose while in subconscious mind as a soul before they are born.

Humanity has evolved a lot through eons of evolution so that the children incarning now are more full of LIGHT and awareness than in the past.

Therefore, these children coming into the physical Earth plane at the present time have a great need to be taught the Universal Truths and Universal Laws from a very early age.

They also need parents that have disciplined minds, are responsible and live according to the Universal Laws and Universal Truths. Indigo and Crystal children need adults that will be honest and not manipulative with them.

Indigo children can see through dishonesty and manipulation instantly.

For the first year of his life, Hezekiah was cared for and taught and raised by Barbara and myself, his Mommy and Daddy.

That first year he was with us as we practiced the still and disciplined mind.

Barbara and I have been practicing and teaching about the mind for over 30 years. We have taught thousands of adults how to discipline their minds and to know Self. We have taught the Universal Laws and Truths. We have taught mental perception and communication skills. We have taught dream interpretation through in-class study to thousands and through media to millions.

Therefore, when our son, Hezekiah, was born we wanted to impart to him our learning, practice and teaching of the mind.

Indigo children instinctively recognize dishonesty and manipulation. I have taught Hezekiah from the time he was born and before he was born with a still and open mind and with an open heart.

Most people do not have an open heart because they live in fear. Fear and doubt also keep people from having an open mind. Mental discipline to produce a still mind is a necessary requirement to developing an open mind and an open heart.

Hezekiah's mind has remained open because I have not allowed other people to squash his spirit.

Anger, hatred, jealousy, manipulation, abuse, dishonesty, resentment and fear all smash a child's spirit and will force him or her to retreat back deep into the Self. This is done for Self protection and Self preservation. In many cases, the child is just attempting to survive.

Hezekiah, who I often call Kie Danny, was never forced to retreat to a survival mode. Therefore, he remained open to the learning.

I taught him every day. What did I teach him? I taught him words, numbers, geography, addition, nature, trees, water, animals, objects, love, happiness, joy, touching, security, trips, openness and a thousand other subjects. ALL in his first year.

Most parents, these days, aren't even home to teach their children. Their first seven years of life, the most crucial years, are given to baby sitters or day care centers or government schools. Yet this is the very time when children need their parents the most.

If children do not have the parents near them in the early years, they will not in most cases, develop the security they need to not only be successful in life but to be enlightened in life.

Success is not enlightenment. Physical success does not necessarily mean you will fulfill your purpose in life. In many, if not most cases, people who are physically successful are not fully fulfilling their purpose in life.

This is because the purpose of life is not physical. So to attempt to fulfill your life's purpose strictly through physical means is doomed to failure.

Since Indigo children and Crystal children are so in tune with their inner purpose they will always want to learn. They will put learning and growth above physical possessions and physical wealth. This is why it is often difficult for physically bound parents to understand their Indigo children. These children identify with the purpose of life more than physical objects.

Physically engrossed and physically minded parents often say to their spiritually-minded, purpose-filled children who have now become young adults, "Why are you volunteering your service? They don't pay you anything." Other times they may say, "How much is that church or not-for-profit paying you?" or "Why are you spending so much time over there when they don't pay you?"

Indigo and Crystal children know better than this. They are mental thinkers. People that ask or say what I have just indicated are physical thinkers.

If you live your life for the physical world then the physical is all you will get. However to know your purpose and fulfill it requires that you master your mind in order to know Self.

A physical thinker knows only the physical brain and the physical world.

The purpose of life concerns much more than your physical body and the five physical senses and your physical possessions.

Indigo and Crystal children know there is a deeper purpose to life and they are going to discover and fulfill that higher and deeper purpose.

This is why Indigo children and Crystal children will not tolerate manipulation and deceit.

At a very early age of two or three years old, Hezekiah would get very angry at any adult who was with him who was not fully honest.

Barbara and I never let people be with him unless they had first taught adults how to improve their lives and improve their minds.

Also those people that did spend time with Hezekiah did so on the College of Metaphysics campus where we reside. So, Kie was never far from Mommy or Daddy. In fact, he was always within shouting distance.

I love my little boy and from the start told him so. I have told him this thousands of times.

I also told him that I like him. I still say to Kie, "I like that little boy. I like him a lot."

I would say things to Kie like, "He's a happy boy!" He was and is a happy boy because children are born happy. They only lose their happiness when taught to do so by the adults in their environment.

I taught Hezekiah love, friendship and happiness. More importantly I taught him to retain those qualities which he already possessed.

I want my son to lead a happy and fulfilling life. Therefore, this is what I teach him.

One day I walked into the Great Room at the College of Metaphysics. There I encountered Hezekiah who was very upset. He was saying in a very adamant way, "Stop saying that Laurie." Laurie was the adult student-teacher who was with him at the time.

Hezekiah repeated loudly, "Stop saying that."

I said, "Hezekiah what is it you want Laurie to stop saying?" to which nine-year-old Hezekiah said, "Laurie says, 'Love hurts'."

I said, "Laurie is that true?"

She said, "Well, love does hurt."

I said, "That is not true. Love does not hurt!"

To which Hezekiah added a resounding, "Yeah!"

I continued, "If you think love hurts, Laurie, then you are confusing something else with love. Love never hurts. It is what people do that isn't love that masquerades as love that sometimes hurts."

Hezekiah was listening to all this and I know he was glad I was there to offer the truth.

Hezekiah knew intuitively and from early education by Barbara and myself that what Laurie was saying was untrue. He just didn't have the words or experience to say why or how it was untrue. All he would do was firmly and strongly tell Laurie to stop saying that. He knew it was a lie.

Sometimes well meaning adults pass on lies and wrong thinking to children because that is the way they were taught as children. That does not make it right, however.

The ideal is for each generation to get better, more loving, wiser and more truth-filled. Rather than just mindlessly or habitually passing on bad habits, wrong thinking and limitations in consciousness.

I was glad I was there to make sure my son was supported, vindicated and encouraged in standing up for the truth. Even if he is nine years young and Laurie, the adult, was almost 30. They are still very good friends, and I got to teach them both. Laurie has never repeated that false phrase again. She continues to grow in love, LIGHT and truth.

Hezekiah will continue to build confidence in teaching and sharing what he knows.

I wonder how many other times well-meaning adults have told him wrong things and have had wrong thinking with Kie when I was not close by. And this by people who have spent years training themselves and their minds. Yet no one is perfect.

I wonder what the children of this country are being taught when the parents work all day, while an inexperienced or experienced babysitter or day care center worker is with them.

Children deserve to be raised by their parents and Indigo and Crystal children perhaps need their parents even more. Because if they are to fulfill their mission of enlightening the planet they must be taught Universal Truth and Universal Love from birth on. I even taught my son, Hezekiah, before he was born both as the physical baby in the mother's womb and as a soul existing in subconscious mind.

Indigo children came first starting in about 1995. Their precursors were exceptionally talented and gifted children.

The Indigo children are the harbingers of a new race of people-beings that are in contact with their inner purpose for life. This is different from the vast majority of people on this planet that don't have a clue as to their purpose in life or the purpose of life.

Next came the Crystal children. This is the evolutionary step of the human race from a carbon-based life form to a crystaline-based life form. I wrote about this phenomenon several years ago in a book I co-authored with my wife Barbara called Atlantis, the History of the World, Volume 1.

Just as coal is transformed through pressure and heat into diamonds, so our carbon-based life form called Homo Sapiens is being transformed by the heat of the expansion of consciousness into Homo Enlightenment or Homo Pure Consciousness or Homo Spiritus.

Drugging children, as is done in government schools, only impedes this natural process. Drugging children with ritalin or other drugs only keeps them from being the greatness they are designed to be. Which, by the way, is much greater than the people who are doing the drugging and promoting the drugging of our wonderful, intelligent, enlightened children.

When I was a child, people were put in prison for pushing drugs in public schools. Now the schools insist on pushing them on our children. These drugs are unnatural. As such, they delay and postpone the learning process that children need in their early formative years.

In order to learn and fulfill their purpose, the child must be allowed to develop naturally, without mind altering substances.

It is of utmost importance that the young children of today be allowed to develop even though they are different than preceding generations. This difference is good and valuable and useful.

Parents need to aid their children in manifesting their potential which may be different from that of their parents or grandparents.

Thought to remember:

Each child is unique and each person is unique. Help each child develop his or her potential.

What to do:

Give your full attention to a child. Answer the child's questions to the fullest of your capabilities.

Chapter 26
Using Words
to Know Your Purpose

Words are a powerful tool for discovering purpose.

Give your full attention to each word you speak. By giving full attention to each word, your thoughts slow down. As the thoughts slow down, you become more aware of your thoughts.

By examining your thoughts, you gain the ability to choose which thoughts you wish to think and which thoughts you wish to discard.

Through this process, you discard such thoughts as anger, resentment, guilt, doubt, hate, envy, jealousy, gossip, confusion, worthlessness and dread.

These negative or limiting thoughts can then be replaced with thoughts of kindness, love, truth, perspective, value, worth, determination, purpose, caring and joy.

This is the process of refining thoughts from the negative to the positive, from the limiting to the expansive, from the senseless and purposeless to the purposeful.

When you are unaware of the words that you are using, then these are the words of which you are unconscious. **In order to progress in understanding your purpose in life, you must become conscious and grow in awareness.**

Words describe thoughts. Therefore, becoming conscious of the words one thinks and speaks enables one to better know one's thoughts. By knowing your thoughts you can more clearly choose thoughts in alignment with your purpose.

The Power of Listening

Sometimes people are thinking about what they are going to say next while they are still talking. Sometimes people think about what they are going to say next while the other person in the conversation is speaking. If you are thinking while the other person is speaking, you are going to miss most of what the other person is saying.

If it is worth your time to have a conversation with another person, it is worth your time to listen to that person.

What is communication? Communication is asking questions and listening. Therefore, to inhibit your ability to listen is to restrict your ability to communicate. To restrict your ability to communicate is to severely limit your ability to receive. To restrict your ability to receive is to limit the opportunities to discover more about your purpose.

To practice thinking about what you will say next before you or the other person is done speaking is to practice fear. This may take the form of fear of being wrong or fear of not winning an argument or fear of losing or fear of being found out or fear of being stupid or of being incompetent or of not remembering what you were going to say.

Giving attention to each word imparts the ability to choose the words necessary to convey an idea and to gain greater Self awareness.

In order to gain a higher calling, a higher purpose, one must learn to give according to a higher truth. This higher truth is called Universal Truth. The individual must be aware of his or her thoughts in order to accomplish this. Living according to Universal Truth enables one to live in harmony with the Universal Laws. Living in harmony with the Universal Laws leads to a more harmonious and purpose-filled life.

Be aware of the words you say. Your words can aid you to identify your own thoughts. In identifying your own thoughts you can discern whether you and your words are limiting or expansive, negative or positive, true or false, closed off or open to learning, aggressive or receptive.

For three years, I gave myself the discipline of not saying nots. In other words, I chose the commitment of stating everything I said positively.

This practice, this discipline, aided me in several ways.

1. First it raised and improved my awareness of my own thoughts.

2. I learned there was more than one way to describe my thoughts.

At times I would begin to habitually say the word *not*. As I caught myself saying *not* or about to say *not*, I would stop talking. Then I would consciously choose to make the statement in another way. This time without the *not*. This taught me that I could say something in more than one way.

3. This in turn gave me more flexibility and command of the English language and my own speaking ability.

4. I strengthened my will.

Because I was exercising my choice-making ability by choosing to say something other than *not*, I was developing a greater will and will power. Will is the ability to make a choice or decision toward a goal or ideal. Will power is the ability to make a series of choices or decisions toward a goal or ideal until success and completion are achieved.

5. I developed a greater commitment to know myself and gain enlightenment.

This continued use of choice, will and willpower, produces greater and greater commitment in the Self. Then the greatest commitment is known and realized in the Self. This is the full commitment to know the Self.

6. Little steps practiced every day lead to great accomplishments.

This discipline further strengthened my understanding that it is the little things, the little disciplines, practiced over and over every day, that lead to the great achievements in life. A little discipline practiced 365 days a year can have a tremendous effect on the outcome of one's life.

7. Greater use of my conscious mind and improved ability to consciously be in the present moment.

Instead of habitually saying the easiest or first words that came to my mind, I had to stop my thinking and deliberately choose a different word. Often I found my description of the thought improved because of this choice and process.

Instead of letting my habits or brain memories control me, I was actually being in the present moment choosing the exact words I wanted to say. I was visualizing my mental picture or thought and choosing words that accurately described this thought.

These are some of the benefits I received from not saying the word *not*. It was a choice, a decision, that I practiced regularly and consistently for over three years.

At the end of the three years my discipline changed. I allowed myself to say the word *not*. However, I only allowed myself to use the word *not* if I was conscious of what I was saying. In other words, before I use the word *not*, I must deliberately choose that word intentionally. There must be a purpose behind using the word.

Nowadays, when I do use the word *not* I usually use it to get someone's attention. Sometimes, I find *not* is most effective in getting people's attention. Then I go on to state my instruction or knowledge exactly the way I image it.

Anyway, there is no such thing as *not*. Just as there is no such thing as a donut hole. A donut hole is the empty place or spot in the middle of a donut. A hole is an empty space. A *not* is an empty space. Just as I identified a donut hole as the empty space in the middle of a donut, so also can a *not* be described in other ways. This I learned to do.

I wrote an explanation of the <u>Tao Te Ching</u> in book form called <u>The Tao Te Ching Interpreted and Explained</u>. Chapter 11 of that book explains the value of space, emptiness and a hole.

> *11*
> *Thirty spokes unite in the hub of the wheel*
> *It is the emptiness of the center w-hole*
> *that makes it useful*
>
> *Shape clay into a bowl*
> *It is the space within that allows it to be useful*
>
> *Cut out doors and windows for a house*
> *these created openings of space give it usefulness*
>
> *Thus, while physical form is beneficial*
> *Its usefulness comes from creating space*

What I was really learning in the discipline of not saying *nots* was the value and usefulness of space and emptiness.

When I chose to not say a *not*, what I was actually doing was emptying my mind of thoughts and creating a space where a higher consciousness could enter. From this I was able to respond in a much more effective way.

Not is a word used to make a statement negative, yet will you or anyone else fulfill their life's purpose by being negative?

The hallmark of a reasoner is adding to what already exits, which is to produce more than you consume.

Not does not add to what already exists. However, receptivity definitely benefits self and those around self.

Receptivity is the ability to still the mind and expect to receive. It is expectant non-action. Far from being passive, receptivity has a definite desire, goal or ideal in mind. Receptivity is not a *not*.

The one who can create space understands the power of receptivity. The one who knows to expectantly listen can receive the truth of the universe. The one who can still the mind, can receive the truth and abundance of the universe.

I also practiced eliminating the word *but* from my vocabulary for some time. What I learned from this discipline is that *but* cancels out what has come before.

For example, if I am talking or explaining a Universal Truth or Universal Principle and someone says "but", I know that person has rejected the Truth I have just offered. That person has refused to receive something new or different. How can you or anyone grow and learn if there is a refusal to receive?

The time of greatest and most rapid learning in our lives is infancy. This is because the baby rejects no learning. The infant completely absorbs all experiences in the environment. Not so with adults. Adults pick and choose what they are willing to hear, listen to and receive. Unfortunately, as people get older, most often they are willing to receive less and less new ideas and new knowledge.

The key to fulfilling life's purpose lies in being about to cause yourself to become more and more open as we grow in years rather than closing off. Closing off of the mind leads to closing off and shutting down of the body. This leads to sickness and eventually lack of choice about when you will withdraw from physical life, which is death.

For a comprehensive list of dis-eases and the attitudes that cause them, see my book <u>Permanent Healing</u>.

Choose to have an open mind and an open heart. Be open to life. Receive the goodness that life affords.

Receiving new thoughts and new ideas into the Self enables the individual to make better choices because more options are known. It also enables one to be a better reasoner because reasoning is a product of memory, attention and imagination.

The one who rejects the communication or instruction in the present as evidenced by the use of the word *but* at the beginning of a sentence, cancels out his or her learning.

In order to learn, one needs to receive. The word *but* at the beginning of a sentence indicates you refuse to receive. The word *but* is a conjunction. A conjunction is intended to join two thoughts. A person that regularly begins sentences with the word *but* while talking with another person usually is living in fear that is of the past.

Why would you reject the present unless you are not in the present moment mentally?

If you have been hurt mentally, emotionally or physically in the past and are attached to this hurt, then that same hurt will color everything you experience in the present. Any person, place or thing that comes into your sphere of perception will be evaluated through the filter of your own preconceptions and biases.

The only place to live is in the present. The only place to grow is in the eternal now.

Therefore, use your words to identify limitations in thinking and consciousness and replace the limited thinking with a greater thought and a higher consciousness.

Thought to remember:
Your words describe your thoughts. Pay attention to them.

What to do:
Give attention to every time you say the words *not* or *but*. Then evaluate. Is there a better way to make your point?

Chapter 27

Dreams and Purpose

Remembering and interpreting dreams is incredibly powerful in aiding anyone to move rapidly and consistently to understand the purpose of life.

Each night's dream is a corrective device for staying on track to fulfill one's life purpose.

Night dreams provide feedback for understanding who you are. Dreams also aid you to know how to be more productive with your mind, your consciousness and your Self.

Dreams are instruction from one's subconscious mind concerning the learning and growth or lack of it in the previous day's activities.

For example, the person moves through a day's experiences and has certain thoughts and attitudes about this. That night the subconscious mind, having processed the experience, gives feedback in the form of a dream.

Why doesn't the subconscious mind give feedback just in words instead of a story? Because the language of the mind is pictures.

I discovered this universal language while a young boy in Sunday School. Each week, I would go to Sunday School and be taught Bible stories by my Sunday School teacher. At the end of each weekly class I was given a magazine comic book called Sunday Pix. It wasn't until years later that I realized that the word Pix stood for pictures.

Each week this Sunday Pix contained one of the Bible stories in comic book form. One day I thought, "Wouldn't it be great to have the whole Bible in pictures!"

So I began to save all those old Sunday Pix with their Bible stories. I put them in an old 3-ring binder, a red notebook that had its front cover worn off. For many years I collected those stories in pictures.

Now I know and teach that the key to all language is pictures. Dreams are a language.

The key to understanding all the great scriptures and myths of the world is pictures.

The ancient written languages before the invention of the alphabet were pictorial languages. Egyptian hieroglyphics as well as Aztec and Mayan writing are given in pictures. The Chinese language is written in pictures. Originally the glyphs looked like the picture they were describing. For example, the written word for *tree* may have looked like a tree or the word *house* looked like a house. This was true for much of the Mayan and Aztec writing. Some of the symbols still do look like their physical counterpart if you know what to look for.

With the introduction of the alphabet, letters and words were substituted for pictures in the written language. Abstract letters were substituted for the exact or literal image.

For example, consider the word *apple*. The written word *apple* does not look like an apple. Yet if you see a picture of an apple you immediately know what the picture means or indicates.

In a similar fashion, if you hear the word *apple*, you may form a mental picture or image of an apple.

We use commonly agreed upon spoken words to describe and identify people, places and things. We use abstract written words to do the same thing.

The subconscious mind or soul does not need to deal in or communicate in abstractions. Your subconscious mind goes straight to the core or essence of what you in the conscious, waking mind need to learn. Therefore, your subconscious mind gives you its communication in the form of dream images.

When two people talk to each other, words are used to describe images. For example, one person forms the image or idea of a tree in the mind. The person then says the word *tree*. The listener hears the word *tree* and forms an image in the mind of a tree.

The subconscious mind, via the dream state, makes things much simpler. The subconscious mind gives you a picture of a tree if an image of a tree is needed in the communication.

Therefore, you will find that dreams are stories in picture form. Sometimes the characters in the dream story will speak. Sometimes they will not speak. It is the pictures in the dream that are of the utmost significance and importance.

Your subconscious mind is like a best friend that offers you, the dreamer, truth every night. In some ways it is amazing that very few people even remember their dreams. It is even more amazing that when dreams are remembered, people give them little or no attention or credence unless the dream happens to be a nightmare.

Yet all dreams are valuable. All night dreams offer insight. All dreams can aid the dreamer to make better choices, better decisions in life. Through making better decisions in life, one feels more fulfilled and is better able to fulfill life's purpose.

If in a dream, you are looking at your hands, this indicates you, the dreamer, are taking stock of purpose in the waking life. The dreamer may have been thinking, "I wonder what is the purpose of my life" or "There has to be more to life than this."

Perhaps at night after reading this book or a portion of this book you may have a dream with hands as the major symbol. Such a dream would indicate your desire and effort to know greater purpose in life and the desire to fulfill your purpose.

Dreams always indicate the present state of the dreamer's awareness and consciousness. This means that the dream you have tonight will be a report on your state of consciousness, your awareness, in the previous day up to the time you went to sleep.

The dreamers thoughts, attitudes, feelings, re-actions, mental discipline and more are all reflected or reported on in nightly dreams.

Once a person realizes just how important dreams are, he or she can immediately begin to use them for greater Self awareness and purpose in the life.

The basic steps for remembering dreams are:

1. Use a dream notebook

A dream notebook is a book or steno pad with blank pages. On the left side of each page you will write your dream. On the right side you will write your interpretation of the dream. The interpretation is based on the symbols in the dream and their meaning.

2. Date the dream notebook each night in preparation for remembering your dream. Write the next morning's date in your dream notebook each night. Write the next morning's date on the notebook because that is when you will be writing the dream.

3. Tell yourself before going to sleep, "I will remember my dream!" The next morning when you awaken, write your dream in your dream notebook. Do this first thing because the memory of the dream will fade rapidly.

4. Once the dream is written on paper it can be interpreted and the knowledge used immediately and throughout the day.

To begin understanding and interpreting your dreams, the following are some keys to get you started.

1. Every dream is about the dreamer. This means your dreams are about you.

2. People in a dream are aspects of the dreamer.

Aspects indicate ways of thinking. Aspects are all the myriad parts of your thinking and consciousness that go into making you who you are. Examples of aspects are love, will, truth, value, discipline, power, perception, communication, knowing.

When interpreting a dream with people in it, look to see if you know these people in your waking life. If you do not know them then this indicates that you do not know and are not aware of these parts of yourself. You need to become aware of all aspects, all parts, of yourself.

If you know the person or people in your dream this means you are aware of these aspects or parts of yourself in the waking state.

Look to see what the people are doing in the dream. Are they violent or peaceful, kind or mean, honest or deceitful, abusive or loving? However these people appear in your dream, that is related to your thoughts and ways of thinking.

If a robbery of a bank occurs in a dream, it does not necessarily mean the dreamer is going to commit the crime of robbing a bank in the waking state. What the dream does indicate is that the dreamer is stealing from the Self.

How can a person steal from self? You steal from yourself every time you refuse to receive the learning in any experience.

If or when a person refuses to give to others then that person will have a difficult time receiving. Instead of receiving, such a person will tend to try to take from life.

The hallmark of a reasoning adult is to produce more than you consume. If you consume more than you produce then someone else in society is carrying your part of the load.

Look to see what you give and have to give to those in your community. Service through giving in a spiritual community goes a long way toward fulfilling one's life purpose.

One who is giving and receiving fully and with balance in the waking life will have dreams of abundance and prosperity.

3. Dream symbols are based on function.

This was the great discovery I made in the late 1980s and wrote about in my book <u>Understanding Your Dreams</u>.

Our physical life and physical world is a universe of form while the Universal Subconscious mind operates more from function.

Dream symbol interpretation, therefore, reflects the use, purpose and function of those symbols in your dreams.

The following are some common dream symbols that I have found appear often in dreams.

car - body - usually the dreamer's physical body

clothes - one's outer expression or presentation - the way we present ourselves to others

house - the mind. First floor - conscious mind. Second floor - subconscious mind. Third floor - superconscious mind.

people - aspects or qualities of the Self

flying - use of imagination and will

feet - spiritual or mental foundation

animals - habits or compulsive ways of thinking

teeth - tools for assimilating the knowledge or learning in each experience

school or college - a way or place of learning in one's consciousness music - caused or created harmony in the mind of the dreamer

food - knowledge that is available to be used in one's life

These symbols will help aid you, the dreamer, to get started in understanding your dreams. Remember, your dreams are about you. They are symbolic. The symbology is based on function.

For example, the function of a car is to transport people from one location to another. This is exactly the function of the physical body. The physical body functions as a vehicle for transporting the individual through life's experiences, from one place to another.

You are a soul inhabiting a physical body. You are not the physical body. The physical body is the vehicle that you, the individual, I AM, inhabit for a lifetime.

For a more thorough explanation of the Mind, see my book Superconscious Meditation: Kundalini and the Understanding of the Whole Mind.

Dreams give the dreamer insight into who he or she is beyond the physical body. This is because dreams come from subconscious mind.

Definition - Dream -
A message or communication from the dreamer's subconscious mind to the dreamer's conscious mind.

At night you go to sleep and the conscious, outer, waking mind shuts down. Then the subconscious or inner mind takes over. When the conscious mind shuts down, we go into sleep. Then the attention of the individual moves into subconscious mind.

Definition - Mind -
   The vehicle the Self experiences in and through for the purpose of gaining enlightenment.

One thing that dreams begin to teach you early on is that you are not a physical body. The teaching is subtle, but it is there. The more you remember your dreams, the better you understand the fact that the physical body and physical life are to be used for learning about the whole Self. In a dream you may be flying through the air (without any aircraft) and feel free as a bird. When you wake up you wish you could fly like that in your waking state. Yet a part of you knows there was truth and a kind of reality to your experience in the dream state. A state and condition of reality far different from mere daydreaming.

You can visualize yourself flying, or you can experience and feel yourself flying in a dream. You will note that the two are far different expressions of experience and energy.

Note in your nightly dreams how you really don't seem to be making very many decisions. You just seem to be going along with whatever the dream affords you.

Believe it or not, this is exactly your consciousness and thinking during the waking state. In other words, night dreams reflect the dreamers state of awareness, will and understanding.

If you go along with the flow of events in the dreamstate, this is exactly what you do in the waking state. You get up in the morning, think some thoughts, eat food, go to work, look forward to getting off work, eat lunch, go home for the day, eat supper, watch television, go to sleep and then get up and do it all over gain the next day.

Where is the will and imagination in that? There is very little will and imagination exercised in this scenario. Yet will and imagination are exactly what is required in order to fulfill life's purpose as well as to gain greater control and understanding in the dreamstate.

In order to create a goal, one needs imagination. In order to visualize one's ideal self, imagination is needed. For any type or kind of view or different creation, imagination is required.

To move you from where you are to a better place inwardly or outwardly, the effective use of will and willpower is required.

Imagination gives direction to the will.

While in the dreamstate, will and imagination are the dreamer's most powerful tools for gaining awareness and use of the dreamstate.

Have you ever noticed how you are kind of unconscious in the dreamstate? Things just seem to happen to you. Well that is reflective of you in the waking state.

Therefore, get control of your life both inwardly and outwardly, consciously and subconsciously. Learn to choose the things you think and do throughout the day. Refuse to go on automatic pilot or habit. Be conscious and awake in all you do.

When you remember a dream upon awakening, write it down immediately. Remember this dream is about you. Look at the dream. Is this dream similar to a dream you have had before? Do you know some of the people in your dream?

If you do not recognize anyone in a dream this means it is time for you to get to know yourself. It is time to begin meditation and concentration exercises so you can know your thoughts and your consciousness.

There is nothing more important and valuable than a disciplined mind because a disciplined mind aids one to wake up to life and consciousness.

Most people exist in their brains. Few people have yet learned to live in their mind. However, more people are beginning to wake up to life and the tremendous potential that exists in each individual to become enlightened.

Remembering and interpreting your dreams that come from subconscious mind is like having a built-in teacher. The subconscious mind is the older and wiser mind. The conscious mind is the younger, less experienced mind.

Therefore, to receive a dream from subconscious mind and to understand the dream's meaning is essentially accessing a very wise, spiritual, master teacher. This inner teacher will guide you and aid you to lead a more productive, growth-filled life of learning to know the Real Self and a higher consciousness.

If an animal is chasing you in a dream this indicates that you are allowing your habits and compulsions to control you and your life.

If an animal was chasing you and trying to attack and hurt you in your waking life then obviously you would not be doing what you want with your life. You would just be trying to survive.

A dream in which a vicious animal is chasing you means you are compulsively or habitually trying to survive. But life is meant to be much more than just surviving. Life is about creating and learning.

In order to create and learn in life, the individual must make choices. She needs to imagine or visualize what she wants to occur rather than just waiting for events to arise and then reacting out of fear or habit.

The mind must be directed by the thinker if the life is to be fulfilling. Since images or pictures are the language of the mind, it is one's mental images that must be directed in order to achieve one's most heartfelt desires.

The will and imagination must be used to create goals and ideals for the Self. Then the mind can be used to create the situations and circumstances the individual needs in order to be able to learn the life lessons needed to fulfill one's purpose in life.

Ask yourself the following question as you go throughout the day, "Am I making a decision now?" or ask, "Am I being habitual?" or "Am I choosing or am I unconscious?"

These questions and their attendant answers will begin to give you a greater awareness about yourself, your consciousness and your life.

In order to improve one's dreams, the dreamer must improve the Self in the waking life. This means making more and better decisions. This means choosing to be the director of your thoughts and mind rather than a passive re-actor.

A car in a dream symbolizes the dreamer's physical body.

If you are driving a car in a dream this indicates you were directing yourself in your physical body in the previous day's experience.

If in a dream you are in the passenger side of the front seat and someone else is driving your car then you were allowing an aspect of yourself to run your life in the previous day's experience.

If you are riding in the back seat of a car while someone else is driving the car then that dream is telling you that you are taking a backseat to some aspect of yourself in your waking life.

The ideal is for the thinker, the individual, to direct all the thousands of aspects of Self. If only one part, one quality, one aspect of Self is directing yourself then you are severely limited in what can be learned and developed in life. There will be a constriction in your ability to fulfill life's purpose.

Therefore, learn to know the whole Self, the Real you.

If in a dream the dreamer is searching but cannot find his or her car, this indicates the dreamer in the waking state needs to be invested in the life. You, the dreamer, need to find and create physical activities that are productive, useful and fulfilling in your life.

Your physical body is your vehicle in your waking life. The body, your vehicle, is designed to be directed by your mind which is designed to be directed by you.

If you are bored with life or daydream a lot then your attention and thoughts are not where your body is. Your mind is somewhere else. Therefore, you are not directing or driving your car-body.

Boats and small airplanes also symbolize your physical body while large ships, large airplanes, passenger trains, and buses indicate a group or organization you are involved with in your waking life.

If your car breaks down or is in a crash, the dream may indicate the dreamer is about to bring on an illness or dis-ease into the physical body. A car that runs out of gas in a dream indicates the dreamer is running out of energy in the waking life. This may be due to poor diet, unproductive thinking and attitudes or improper breathing among other reasons.

You can learn a lot from the cars in your dreams.

Being the older and wiser, your subconscious mind wants you and the conscious mind to progress and grow. This the subconscious mind knows how to do. The conscious mind does not. **Your conscious mind does not automatically know how to fulfill your purpose because it is young and immature.**

The subconscious mind does know how to fulfill your life's purpose because your subconscious mind in all its wisdom created your life's purpose.

Another way of saying this is, you as a soul created your life's purpose. However, while maturing from an infant to adult you forgot this purpose as most people do.

Remembering dreams enables one to receive and remember one's purpose, one's soul purpose, one's subconscious purpose for a lifetime. What could be more important than that? And dreams are such a quick and easy way to access one's subconscious mind.

Clothes in a dream indicate the dreamer's outer presentation. If you are wearing no clothes and find yourself naked in a dream this will symbolize your greater desire and willingness to open up to life. You may be uncomfortable with opening up. Thus, in the dream you find yourself embarrassed about being naked.

Perhaps the dreamer has learned meditation and this is aiding this one to open up. Perhaps the dreamer has begun a course of study of the mind and Self to open up. Perhaps the dreamer has begun a course of study of the mind and Self with others of like mind and is, therefore, opening up and sharing thoughts and feelings more easily.

When a dream is given in which the dreamer finds the Self inappropriately attired, it is a message saying the dreamer needs to change the outer expression in the waking, day to day life. Perhaps you are too harsh or too gruff or too passive and weak or callous and unkind or refuse to listen to others. Maybe you need more love or truth in the words and emotions you share with others.

If in a dream the dreamer needs a second set of clothes but does not have them, there is an indication that the individual needs to be more flexible in the way he or she expresses and presents the Self to others. You are being too one-dimensional. Therefore, open up and learn to share the many facets of Self with others.

A house symbolizes the dreamer's mind. The first floor of a house symbolizes the conscious, waking mind of the dreamer. The second floor of a house symbolizes the subconscious mind. The third floor or attic of a house symbolizes the dreamer's superconscious mind.

The basement of a house will symbolize the unconscious part of the brain of the dreamer.

People often confuse the words *unconscious* and *subconscious*. Some people even use them interchangeably. However, they are not the same.

The brain is a physical organ in the physical body. The brain stores memories. Sometimes some of these memories are unpleasant and relate to hurt or pain the person suffered as a child. In an effort to cope and survive, the person suppressed these memories and so became unconscious of them. The memories of these experiences are then stored in the unconscious part of the brain, but the person is no longer conscious or aware of these memories In other words, he or she no longer remembers these unpleasant experiences.

Yet they remain, causing the person to re-act in the strangest way and in the most inopportune times. They produce self defeating actions and behavior.

Until the person is willing to draw forth those unconscious memories to examine them in the light of reason, they will remain just below the surface of waking consciousness, causing the person to re-act as if the present is the past.

When one dreams of being in the basement of a house, the solution or meaning is to bring your attention to the present while in the waking state. Stop dwelling in the past and begin living and being in the present moment. Appreciate the present moment for what it is, a time of learning and joy.

When dreaming of being on the first floor of a house, recognize the subconscious mind is presenting an image concerning the dreamer's conscious mind.

The conscious mind is that part or division of mind the individual uses in the waking state. The conscious mind is designed to direct the physical brain, although most people do not know how to do this.

The conscious mind works with the brain and five senses of sight, hearing, taste, touch and smell to explore and learn about the world around us.

The conscious mind uses memory, attention and imagination to build the ability to reason. Memory is used to draw forth images from one's past to apply in one's present experience.

Attention is applied and practiced in the present to fully receive and know the life lessons available in the present moment.

Imagination, the ability to visualize and image the possible future, gives one the ability to direct the mind toward goals, ideals and purposes. The ideal and goal may manifest or come to fruition tomorrow, the next day, next week, next month or next year.

Therefore, with memory, attention and imagination, one has the ability to use the conscious mind to the fullest to reason.

Reasoning is the Power of the Conscious Mind.

It is the use of memory, attention and imagination that enables one to solve problems.

1. The average person lives mostly in their memories of the past.
2. The exceptional individual is able to access and use the imaging faculty successfully.
3. The enlightened being employs the mental discipline of concentration and meditation to achieve life in the present moment. Since the present is the only time that exists, the individual with a still mind gains the greatest soul growth and spiritual development from each and every experience.

Your subconscious mind is your inner teacher. Dreams come from subconscious mind. If you are on the second floor of a house in your dream, this indicates your subconscious mind is informing you about your use or lack of use of subconscious mind while in the waking, conscious state.

All dreams are about the thoughts, attitudes and awareness in the conscious mind. Dreams come from your subconscious mind.

Your subconscious mind will always present true, factual knowledge. The subconscious mind presents truth to the conscious mind in the form of dreams. It is you, the dreamer's responsibility to learn the means and method of this mind to mind communication. This book serves the purpose of helping you, the dreamer, to fulfill that purpose.

If you dream of being in a very large house, the symbolic meaning is the expansive possibilities of using your mind.

If in a dream you are trapped in a haunted house, this indicates you are attached to the past, live in fear based on the past and need to move your attention to the present day and moment.

Giving your full attention to the present moment will give you the opportunity to experience more of life and use more of your mind. Therefore, you will no longer have haunted house dreams.

If in a dream you are moving into a beautiful house that is larger than the one you had before, then in your waking state you are using your mind in greater ways than you have ever done before.

When you, the dreamer, dream of building a new house, this symbolizes that you are building the ability to use your mind in new ways. Your whole consciousness is changing.

Early in my studies of disciplining my mind and developing my consciousness, I had a dream about my physical father's house.

In the dream, I was in my old room. It was the room that my brother and I used growing up. The room was on the second floor, the upstairs of the house.

In the dream the house was on fire. I was attempting to remove the things of value from my room on the second floor as the fire was burning around me. The interesting thing about this fire was it was taking a long time to burn. The fire was burning slowly even though it was all throughout the house. Therefore, I had time to remove those possessions that I still wanted from the house.

The symbols in this dream are:

1. my father's house = my mind
2. my father = superconscious aspect
3. second floor = subconscious mind
4. possessions and valuables = value in my consciousness
5. fire = expansion of consciousness

This is the meaning of the dream based upon the interpretation of the symbols.

1. I am learning to use my mind more productively.
2. I am discovering the tremendous value stored in subconscious mind.
3. My consciousness is expanding.
4. I am preparing for a greater use of my mind.
5. I am aligning with the divine plan for me to be enlightened using more of superconscious mind.

This dream was brought about due to my efforts to discipline my conscious mind and align my conscious and subconscious minds. I am recognizing the value of the permanent learning, the understandings that I have built. I intend to continue to use this expansion of consciousness in my life.

The attic of a house and the third floor of a house symbolize one's superconscious mind.

The superconscious mind holds the blueprint for you to become a whole, functioning self, an enlightened being.

The superconscious mind provides life force to all the rest of mind, the subconscious and conscious minds. Therefore, hold in mind your image of your ideal, enlightened, loving, LIGHT and truth filled Self and become that Real Self.

People in a dream represent aspects of the dreamer.

If the people in your dream have no faces, this means you

have yet to determine who you are, your true identity.

If all the people in the dream are female or all male, the dream will indicate that you, the dreamer, are not in balance. Either you are giving all your attention to your subconscious mind or all of your attention to your conscious mind.

In night dreams, people of the same sex as the dreamer indicate conscious mind aspects. People of the opposite sex symbolize subconscious aspects.

If people refuse to talk to you in a dream, this is a part of yourself you have closed off to your own awareness.

If there are few people in your dream, it can indicate you are learning to still your mind.

When the dreamer is afraid of the people in the dream or the people are violent, then a part of the dreamer's thoughts are out of control, undisciplined or not aligned with LIGHT, love and truth. When in the dream you find yourself with kind, loving people that you can learn and share with, then in your waking life the previous day, you, the dreamer, had kind and loving thoughts and attitudes.

Flying in a dream symbolizes the dreamer's use of will and imagination applied to go beyond self conceived limitations.

When flying in a dream people usually feel an exhilaration and freedom unlike anything on the earthly plane of existence. We can also approach this feeling of flying when we go beyond our preconceived limitations to achieve greatness in the life.

Think about this. What is it that you really want to do, achieve or complete but have been putting off for a long time?

Now do it. Whatever it takes, get it done. Fulfill the mission you have given yourself. Complete it. Then you will fly in your dreams.

Feet provide the body with a physical foundation. Predominant feet in a dream indicate one's spiritual or mental

foundation. This is the function of feet.

When in a dream your feet are bare and you are looking at them, the meaning is you are considering and examining your spiritual foundation in your waking life. You may be wondering what is life really all about. You may have begun to practice mental discipline in order to align your conscious and subconscious minds and thereby know your mental foundation.

As you build greater discipline of the mind, the spiritual foundation in the conscious mind becomes stronger. As you practice meditation, your spiritual foundation becomes stronger and more clear to you. As you remember, interpret and apply your dreams in your waking life, your mental foundation becomes stronger.

Shoes on your feet in a dream indicate the dreamer has developed ways to protect his or her spiritual foundation. This can be productive if one is holding fast to quickening one's soul growth and opening up to learning. If, however, this protection is based on fear and one closes off to the world, then this will be to one's detriment. Therefore, give attention to the growth of the whole Self, discipline the mind, expand the consciousness, open up and grow in awareness.

Allowing brain pathways or habits to control one's life can lead to a dream with animals in it. The animals can be gentle or they can be ferocious.

If the dreamer is playing with small animals in a dream, the symbolic meaning is the dreamer is giving a lot of attention to brain pathways and limited thinking. There is usually a lack of imagination and reasoning as well.

A dream of a large, vicious animal attacking or chasing the dreamer means the dreamer is allowing habits to control and rule the life and the thinking. This will not lead to a satisfying purpose-filled life. Therefore, approach each day as a new opportunity for life. Think new thoughts, eliminate negative thoughts and come to know your purpose.

Food in a dream symbolizes knowledge. Just as physical food nourishes our physical body so does knowledge of the Self nourish our subconscious mind.

When a dream is experienced wherein the dreamer is at a banquet table eating rich fare, the meaning is the dreamer has been learning and receiving great knowledge in the waking state the day before.

The dream you dream at night reflects your consciousness, thoughts and reactions of the previous day.

A dream in which the dreamer is sitting at a banquet table with everyone eating except the dreamer has a different meaning. This dream indicates the dreamer has lots of opportunities for learning yet is refusing to receive and use them. Such a one is wasting valuable opportunities for Self knowledge and self awareness.

The quality of food in the dream will symbolize the quality and degree of self knowledge one is gaining in the waking life.

Teeth in a dream symbolize tools for assimilating the knowledge or learning in each experience.

A dream of one's teeth falling out symbolizes one's inability or refusal to receive the learning or knowledge in the previous day's experience. This is a common dream.

The solution to this dream is to make a commitment to having an open mind to learning new and deeper truths about life and the Self.

A school or college in a dream symbolizes a way of learning or a place of learning in one's consciousness.

A frequent dream concerning school or college is the following:

The dreamer is on a college campus and is a student there. The dreamer is walking across campus and all of a sudden realizes it is the last day of the semester, and he is walking to take the final exam. The problem, the dreamer realizes, is that he hasn't studied all semester and is not ready or prepared to take the test. This produces a feeling of anxiety, fear or dread in the dreamer in the dream.

The meaning of this dream is that there are learning opportunities in the waking life, but the individual is not taking daily, disciplined steps to gain the learning needed. Therefore, he is not prepared to pass the tests that life holds for him.

The remedy for this kind of dream is to choose to use each day's experience to the fullest. The dreamer needs to open up, learn and gain the greatest knowledge and awareness in those experiences. Choose new experiences that provide challenges to reach and go beyond limitations.

No one ever gained enlightenment by being comfortable. Life is a stretch. Life is for reaching.

Challenge yourself each day to reach, to stretch and to learn about yourself in all situations. The discipline needed to receive the learning in all experiences aids one to fulfill the purpose of life.

Music symbolizes harmony within the mind of the individual. Harmony is created or caused when the individual in the waking state harmonizes her mind with the minds of others and with the experience.

The attitude of cooperation and working together with others helps to produce this harmony within the mind of the individual.

Harmony can be developed by oneself in meditation. Yet, in order for harmony to fully exist in one's consciousness permanently, it must be practiced with others of like mind.

Harmony within the mind aids one to fulfill life's purpose by aligning the conscious and subconscious minds. This enables one to open up both to the learning in the outer environment and the messages the subconscious mind conveys. Repeating an affirmation or Holy word over and over can produce harmony in the mind.

Dreams provide anyone instant access to communication, feedback and instruction from their subconscious mind.

It takes commitment to be wiling to write your dream down each morning upon arising.

Even greater commitment is required to learn to interpret your dreams.

Even greater commitment is required to apply the interpretation, the instruction, in your daily life.

Even greater commitment is required to teach others to understand the messages their dreams offer.

The daily interpretation of night dreams will enable one to stay on track to fulfill one's life purpose. The subconscious mind will always guide the way for the conscious mind that is willing to listen, receive and apply.

Thought to consider:

Dreams are a powerful tool to aid one to know Self and the purpose of life.

What to do:

Buy a steno book or journal with blank pages. Begin remembering and recording your dreams. Seek out a teacher that can teach you to understand the meaning of your dreams.

Chapter 28
Summary: Commitment and Purpose

Commitment is the one factor that often determines success or failure in any endeavor.

Until one is fully committed to a goal, ideal or endeavor there is vacillation, distraction and hesitation.

> **Commitment is the factor that has enabled me to write this book.**
>
> **Commitment is the factor that caused me to gain the experience, knowledge, learning and growth needed to write this book.**
>
> **Commitment is the factor needed to discover and fulfill your purpose in life.**

You choose to be on Earth in a physical body for a specific purpose. You will only be satisfied when you are fulfilling your life's purpose.

We all have the general purpose of becoming enlightened and like our Creator.

In addition, each one of us has a specific purpose for this lifetime we choose. This is what makes life so fun and exciting.

Each person has something unique and valuable to learn and understand within the Self.

In addition, each individual has something valuable and unique to give to the world. You have yourself to give to the world. You have your learning, knowledge, wisdom and understanding to give to the world.

The more you progress and gain enlightenment the more LIGHT, love and truth you have available to offer the world.

There is no end to learning, and there is no end to giving. Because there is no end to giving, there is no end to receiving. It is only when one stops giving that he or she stops learning. This is because giving initiates the cycle of giving and receiving.

One of the Holy Books, the Bible says, "As you give, so you shall receive." This is certainly true. As you give of your time, energy, and effort, you open yourself up to receive from the abundance of the universe.

It has been said that "nature abhors a void." Therefore, when you give you create a space or void or opening within the Self that allows nature, the universe or subconscious mind to fill or fulfill.

Be committed to not only getting or receiving but also to giving. This is why service is so important in the fulfillment of purpose.

To be committed to fulfilling life's purpose requires a disciplined mind. A disciplined mind leads to and develops a still mind. The still mind can align conscious and subconscious minds to know one's purpose.

Forming an ideal of what one wants to become and a goal of what is desired to be accomplished enables one to fulfill the realization or discovery of one's purpose.

An outer purpose benefits one physically. An inner purpose benefits one spiritually. Thus, the true and greatest purpose always benefits the inner Self and the whole Self, for people are mental, emotional and physical beings. They are not just physical. Therefore, to live a life just for physical purposes will never bring lasting fulfillment. Instead, focus on and be committed to the understanding that is permanent and lasting.

Gratitude and forgiveness aid one to update and be in the present. Thus, they facilitate the commitment to permanent and lasting understanding and fulfillment of one's life purpose.

Imagination and choice are invaluable in aiding one to fulfill the soul urge or purpose. In order to have commitment one must imagine the commitment and what will be required to fulfill the commitment. Then the choice-maker, the decision-maker, must be repeatedly employed to form a will power that will move one to the fulfillment of the commitment of Self awareness and understanding of life.

When one imagines and receives a clear image of the greatness one can achieve then the ego will motivate the self to achieve these great rewards.

The conscious mind must be developed and disciplined in order to direct the brain and conscious ego productively. Then the brain, the conscious ego and conscious mind can work together effectively to fulfill the commitment to achieve the enlightenment of the whole Self.

Making conscious choices enables one to go beyond the compulsive brain to access the mind. The choice to exercise one's imagination also enables one to go beyond pre-conceived ideas, and therefore, use the mind.

Most of the time when people are stuck in the brain, it is the reccurring memories that absorb most of their attention. The solution, therefore, is to discipline the mind to enable the Self to remain in the present until there is a specific choice to move the attention.

There are two kinds of desires.
1. Desires based on reaction to environmental stimulus
2. Desires proceeding from self-created purpose

Purpose-created desires enable one to be self motivated and to pursue one's innermost and highest desires.

Purpose-created desires are necessary to develop full commitment.

The three factors necessary for any success are:
1. Ideal
2. Purpose
3. Activity

All three factors are necessary for commitment to function well in the life of the individual.

Activity or action on your desires places you in a position to have the experiences necessary to understand and fulfill your commitment to learning and growth.

Because we exist in a physical body, we need effort, action, motion or activity to produce the whole learning of Universal Law and Universal Truths. Activity moves a person to the place or position or experience necessary to enable one to receive the learning or lesson needed.

If you want to become good at anything, you must practice. If you want to become a good lecturer, then you must practice lecturing. If you want to become a good swimmer, then you practice swimming. Therefore, activity is indispensable for success in any endeavor. Even speaking or talking is an activity and can help build commitment in Self.

Practicing purpose helps one build enlightenment. Purpose is personal benefit. The highest benefit one can receive is enlightenment, which is to enter the Kingdom of Heaven. So practicing and developing purpose in everything you do leads to a quickening and adding to of one's mental and spiritual growth. Each small step fulfilled in life's purpose brings one greater enlightenment.

It is the little steps of purpose, the little steps of enlightenment, practiced each day consistently that lead to the great enlightenment.

Purpose practiced once a day for 100 days is much more powerful than purpose practiced 100 times for one day.

It is the little things we do each day consistently that make the big things happen.

It is the little purposes practiced each day regularly that lead to the fulfillment of life's purpose and the achievement of en-LIGHT-en-ment.

The Process of Creation and the Fulfillment of Purpose

The conscious mind images desires. The subconscious mind receives the desires of the conscious mind and attempts to fulfill them. The conscious mind builds new understandings of Self and creation through receiving the essence of the learning in the physical experience and the manifestation of physical desires. The subconscious mind receives and stores understandings of Self and creation from the conscious mind.

The mind is the vehicle to know the Self. Therefore, all fulfilling purposes will employ either the conscious, subconscious or superconscious minds. A great purpose will fulfill all three divisions of mind.

The purpose of the conscious mind is to receive and gather permanent understandings of Self through one's experiences.

The purpose of the subconscious mind is to store those understandings permanently, thereby making them available to the individual.

The purpose of the superconscious mind is to receive the fulfillment of the divine plan of creation. As the evolved individual progresses, this plan is fulfilled.

To accomplish this fulfillment one must overcome limitations. These may be limitations in one's outer environment. However, ultimately, they are limitations in one's own consciousness. Therefore, it is important to accept no limitations in one's thinking or one's outer life. When a challenge presents itself, the individual should rise to the occasion going beyond comfort or fear to be committed to fulfilling his or her duty. Often this duty is service. It may be the service of cleaning a church or school or organization of a friend's house. It may be the service of lecturing and teaching to aid a service organization to grow.

Service benefits not only the ones being served. Service also benefits the one serving. For as you give, so shall you receive. It is no coincidence that the great enlightened masters of the world, such as Jesus the Christ and Gautama the Buddha, are known as world saviors.

To save anyone from their sins is to uplift their consciousness from mistakes. Thereby the student thinks greater thoughts. From those greater and enlightened thoughts come better decisions and choices that elevate one above past mistakes or errors in judgement. As more and more people are committed to serve by teaching others to grow in awareness, an enlightened planet is achieved.

Love is important to achieve an open mind, an open heart and fulfill life's purpose. For without openness one can never receive the universal lessons that life affords. Love keeps a person open to receive the truth. When truth and love are together, purpose and enlightenment can thrive.

Those who live in fear, anger, resentment or hatred learn and change slowly because they are closed off to life. Those who love life and love people are open to the learning and open to giving and receive the joys of life. Thus one's purpose is fulfilled. Commit yourself to causing no more hurt to yourself and others. Instead be committed to bringing more love into the world.

Concentration and meditation are necessary to fulfill one's purpose in this lifetime. This is because only a disciplined conscious mind can discern and receive the subconscious mind or soul's purpose.

A disciplined mind is an open mind, whereas fear is the

product of an undisciplined mind. Fear will close one off to the love, truth and LIGHT of life.

The <u>Bible</u> is very helpful in fulfilling life's purpose because the <u>Bible</u> is a textbook for knowing the whole mind.

Those who study the <u>Bible</u> with an ideal of learning the deeper purpose of life will find it gives excellent insight.

If you would like to learn this deeper symbolic language in the <u>Bible</u> read my book, <u>The Universal Language of Mind, the Book of Matthew Interpreted</u>. This book will assist you greatly in understanding the deeper truths of the Bible and of your purpose in life. It will help you understand commitment to Self.

The Kundalini creative energy is necessary to unlock the secret of the purpose of your life. Have you ever noticed that when you are creating you feel fulfilled? The use of the Kundalini can assist in all creative endeavors including creating your ideal, enlightened or spiritual self.

The Kundalini energy resides at the base of the spine. When it rises, one experiences flashes of illumination that lead one to a greater purpose in life. Use the flashes of illumination to become more committed to fulfilling your life's purpose.

Karma is the universal life lesson coming at you in your physical life due to the Universal Laws.

Karma is relieved by understanding. Therefore, one who has a purpose of receiving the learning in each life experience will quicken their progression.

Dharma is the duty one owes that is fulfilled by giving and teaching others Universal Truth. When one realizes that, the one who gives the greatest receives the greatest, then purpose becomes fulfilling.

You benefit when you give. You learn when you teach. You further your own progress when you aid others in their progress and development of the whole mind. The greatest giving is to teach and aid others to quicken their soul or mental growth to enlightenment and fulfilling life's purpose. This is the ultimate Dharma.

Commit yourself to doing your duty. Live your dharma which will aid you to fulfill your life's purpose.

To exist in the physical world, in a physical body, you must breathe. Therefore, in order to fulfill your purpose it is very important to learn to breathe properly.

Not only can you breathe air, you can also breathe life force that is in the air and in everything around us. Because everything is alive, everything has life force. Life force from superconscious mind animates everything in the physical universe.

Therefore, it is vitally important to learn to draw upon the storehouse of life force energy. Proper breathing techniques enable one to breathe in life force to a much higher degree and in greater quantities than the average person who is unaware of the existence of life force.

By drawing in extra life force and by learning to breathe correctly, one has more energy to fulfill life's purpose. One can remain active and enlivened all one's life. Be committed to using breath correctly.

To aid others, it is important to learn to listen to your own words. The words you use describe your thoughts. In order to fulfill your purpose, you are going to have to know your thoughts.

When a person does not know his or her thoughts, then he or she does not know the Real Self. Learn to listen to yourself and others.

Do not be a gossip, for gossip destroys. When you feel the need to criticize another and gossip, instead point the finger at yourself and start talking about all your own shortcomings or mistakes. This usually stops gossips. Gossips are not your friends. Therefore, learn to use your words productively in order to fulfill your life's purpose.

Use your night dreams as a special instruction to know yourself in new ways and more deeply than you ever have before. Receive the inner truths to help you know your purpose.

Most of all be committed to knowing your Real Self, who you really are, and your purpose in life.

Everyone has something of value to give to the world. Discovering your purpose will enable you to give your best to the world and fulfill your highest aspirations.

Be committed to this. Strive to know and fulfill your purpose more and more each day. You can become enlightened. You can know I AM. You can fulfill your purpose. Cause it to happen.

Thought to remember:

There is a purpose to my life. I Am committed to knowing and fulfilling my purpose.

What to do:

Say out loud every day: I will know and fulfill my purpose.

Use the knowledge in this book to help you fulfill your purpose.

Now that you know how to learn the purpose of life, pass it on to others.

About the Author

Throughout this lifetime, Daniel R. Condron has strived to understand the secrets of life and to explain them in a form that is understandable to all. He first accomplished this as a young boy when he gained a connectedness with nature being in the woods and pastures while growing up on the family farm in northwest Missouri. He has devoted his life to understanding what is permanent, lasting, knowing the true reality, and the purpose of life. This he teaches to others through the understanding of the still mind. He resides with his wife Barbara and son Hezekiah on the campus of the College of Metaphysics.

Additional titles available from SOM Publishing include:

Dharma: Finding Your Soul's Purpose by Dr. Laurel Clark
ISBN: 0944386-34-2 $10.00

The Wisdom of Solomon by Dr. Barbara Condron
ISBN: 094438633-4 $15.00

Every Dream is about the Dreamer by Dr. Barbara Condron
ISBN: 0944386-27-X $13.00

Peacemaking:
9 Lessons for Changing Yourself, Relationships, & World
Dr. Barbara Condron   ISBN: 0944386-31-8 $12.00

The Tao Te Ching Interpreted & Explained
Dr. Daniel R. Condron ISBN: 0944385-30-x $15.00

How to Raise an Indigo Child
Dr. Barbara Condron   ISBN: 0944386-29-6 $14.00

Atlantis: The History of the World Vol. 1
Drs. Daniel & Barbara Condron ISBN: 0944386-28-8 $15.00

Karmic Healing by Dr. Laurel Clark
ISBN: 0944386-26-1 $15.00

The Bible Interpreted in Dream Symbols - Drs. Condron, Condron, Matthes, Rothermel   ISBN: 0944386-23-7 $18.00

Spiritual Renaissance
Elevating Your Conciousness for the Common Good
Dr. Barbara Condron   ISBN: 0944386-22-9 $15.00

Superconscious Meditation
Kundalini & Understanding the Whole Mind
Dr. Daniel R. Condron   ISBN 0944386-21-0 $13.00

First Opinion: Wholistic Health Care in the 21st Century
Dr. Barbara Condron   ISBN 0944386-18-0 $15.00

The Dreamer's Dictionary by Dr. Barbara Condron
ISBN 0944386-16-4 $15.00

The Work of the Soul
Dr. Barbara Condron, ed. ISBN 0944386-17-2 $13.00

Uncommon Knowledge: Past Life & Health Readings
Dr. Barbara Condron, ed. ISBN 0944386-19-9 $13.00

The Universal Language of Mind
The Book of Matthew Interpreted by Dr. Daniel R. Condron
ISBN 0944386-15-6 $13.00

Permanent Healing
Dr. Daniel R. Condron   ISBN 0944386-12-1 $13.00

Dreams of the Soul - The Yogi Sutras of Patanjali
Dr. Daniel R. Condron   ISBN 0944386-11-3 $9.95

Kundalini Rising: Mastering Your Creative Energies
Dr. Barbara Condron   ISBN 0944386-13-X $13.00

To order write:
                 School of Metaphysics
                 World Headquarters
                 163 Moon Valley Road
                 Windyville, Missouri 65783   U.S.A.

Enclose a check or money order payable in U.S. funds to SOM with
any order. Please include $4.00 for postage and handling of books,
$8 for international orders.

A complete catalogue of all book titles, audio lectures and courses,
and videos is available upon request.

Visit us on the Internet at *http://www.som.org*
e-mail: som@som.org

About the School of Metaphysics

We invite you to become a special part of our efforts to aid in enhancing and quickening the process of spiritual growth and mental evolution of the people of the world. The School of Metaphysics, a not-for-profit educational and service organization, has been in existence for three decades. During that time, we have taught tens of thousands directly through our course of study in applied metaphysics. We have elevated the awareness of millions through the many services we offer. If you would like to pursue the study of mind and the transformation of Self to a higher level of being and consciousness, you are invited to write to us at the School of Metaphysics World Headquarters in Windyville, Missouri 65783.

*The heart of the School of Metaphysic*s is a four-tiered course of study in understanding the mind in order to know the Self. Lessons introduce you to the Universal Laws and Truths which guide spiritual and physical evolution. Consciousness is explored and developed through mental and spiritual disciplines which enhance your physical life and enrich your soul progression. For every concept there is a means to employ it through developing your own potential. Level One includes concentration, visualization (focused imagery), meditation, and control of life force and creative energies, all foundations for exploring the multidimensional Self.

*As experts in the Universal Language of Min*d, we teach how to remember and understand the inner communication received through dreams. We are the sponsors of the National Dream Hotline®, an annual educational service offered the last weekend in April. Study centers are located throughout the Midwestern United States. If there is not a center near you, you can receive the first series of lessons through correspondence with a teacher at our headquarters.

For those desiring spiritual renewal, weekends at our Moon Valley Ranch on the College of Metaphysics campus in the Midwest U.S. offer calmness and clarity. Full Spectrum™ training is given during these Spiritual Focus Weekends. Each weekend focuses on intuitive research done specifically for you in your presence. More than a traditional class or seminar, these gatherings are experiences in multidimensional awareness of who you are, why you are here, where you came from, and where you are going.

The Universal Hour of Peace was initiated by the School of Metaphysics on October 24, 1995 in conjunction with the 50th anniversary of the United Nations. We believe that peace on earth is an idea whose time has come. To realize this dream, we invite you to join with others throughout the world by dedicating your thoughts and actions to peace for one hour beginning at 11:30 p.m. December 31st into the first day of January each year. Living peaceably begins by thinking peacefully. The hour is highlighted with recitation of the *Universal Peace Covenant* (see next page) a document written by over two dozen spiritual teachers. Each year, we encourage people around the world to read the *Covenant* as they welcome the new year. During this time, students and faculty at the College of Metaphysics hold a 24 hour peace vigil in the world's Peace Dome. For more visit www.peacedome.org .

There is the opportunity to aid in the growth and fulfillment of our work. Donations supporting the expansion of the School of Metaphysics' efforts are a valuable way for you to aid humanity. As a not-for-profit publishing house, SOM Publishing is dedicated to the continuing publication of research findings that promote peace, understanding and good will for all of Mankind. It is dependent upon the kindness and generosity of sponsors to do so. Authors donate their work and receive no royalties. We have many excellent manuscripts awaiting a benefactor.

One hundred percent of the donations made to the School of Metaphysics are used to expand our services. The world's first Peace Dome located on our college campus was funded entirely by individual contributions. Presently, donations are being received for the Octagon an international center for multidimensional living. Donations to the School of Metaphysics are tax-exempt under 501(c)(3) of the Internal Revenue Code. We appreciate your generosity. With the help of people like you, our dream of a place where anyone desiring Self awareness can receive education in mastering the mind, consciousness, and the Self will become a reality.

We send you our Circle of Love.

The Universal Peace Covenant

Peace is the breath of our spirit. It wells up from within the depths of our being to refresh, to heal, to inspire.

Peace is our birthright. Its eternal presence exists within us as a memory of where we have come from and as a vision of where we yearn to go.

Our world is in the midst of change. For millennia, we have contemplated, reasoned, and practiced the idea of peace. Yet the capacity to sustain peace eludes us. To transcend the limits of our own thinking we must acknowledge that peace is more than the cessation of conflict. For peace to move across the face of the earth we must realize, as the great philosophers and leaders before us, that all people desire peace. We hereby acknowledge this truth that is universal. Now humanity must desire those things that make for peace.

We affirm that peace is an idea whose time has come. We call upon humanity to stand united, responding to the need for peace. We call upon each individual to create and foster a personal vision for peace. We call upon each family to generate and nurture peace within the home. We call upon each nation to encourage and support peace among its citizens. We call upon each leader, be they in the private home, house of worship or place of labor, to be a living example of peace for only in this way can we expect peace to move across the face of the earth.

World Peace begins within ourselves. Arising from the spirit peace seeks expression through the mind, heart, and body of each individual. Government and laws cannot heal the heart. We must transcend whatever separates us. Through giving love and respect, dignity and comfort, we come to know peace. We learn to love our neighbors as we love ourselves bringing peace into the world. We hereby commit ourselves to this noble endeavor.

Peace is first a state of mind. Peace affords the greatest opportunity for growth and learning which leads to personal happiness. Self-direction promotes inner peace and therefore leads to outer peace. We vow to heal ourselves through forgiveness, gratitude, and prayer. We commit to causing each and every day to be a fulfillment of our potential, both human and divine.

Peace is active, the motion of silence, of faith, of accord, of service. It is not made in documents but in the minds and hearts of men and women. Peace is built through communication. The open exchange of ideas is necessary for discovery, for well-being, for growth, for progress whether within one person or among many. We vow to speak with sagacity, listen with equanimity, both free of prejudice, thus we will come to know that peace is liberty in tranquillity.

Peace is achieved by those who fulfill their part of a greater plan. Peace and security are attained by those societies where the individuals work closely to serve the common good of the whole. Peaceful coexistence between nations is the reflection of man's inner tranquillity magnified. Enlightened service to our fellowman brings peace to the one serving, and to the one receiving. We vow to live in peace by embracing truths that apply to us all.

Living peaceably begins by thinking peacefully. We stand on the threshold of peace-filled understanding. We come together, all of humanity, young and old of all cultures from all nations. We vow to stand together as citizens of the Earth knowing that every question has an answer, every issue a resolution. As we stand, united in common purpose, we hereby commit ourselves in thought and action so we might know the power of peace in our lifetimes.

Peace be with us all ways. May Peace Prevail On Earth.

created by teachers in the School of Metaphysics 1996-7

Notes for each chapter

Chapter 1

Chapter 2

Chapter 3

Chapter 4

Chapter 5

Chapter 6

Chapter 7

Notes for each chapter

Chapter 8

Chapter 9

Chapter 10

Chapter 11

Chapter 12

Chapter 13

Chapter 14

Notes for each chapter

Chapter 15

Chapter 16

Chapter 17

Chapter 18

Chapter 19

Chapter 20

Chapter 21

Notes for each chapter

Chapter 22

Chapter 23

Chapter 24

Chapter 25

Chapter 26

Chapter 27

Chapter 28